はしがき

　本書は第一学習社発行の英語教科書「Vivid English Communication Ⅲ」に完全準拠したワークブックです。本課は各パート見開き2ページで，教科書本文を使って「聞く」「読む」「話す（やり取り）」「話す（発表）」「書く」の4技能5領域の力を育成する問題をバランスよく用意しました。

本書の構成と利用

JN102751

【教科書本文】

- ●新出単語を太字で示しました。
- ●意味のまとまりごとにスラッシュを入れました。ここで示した意味のまとまりや，英語の強弱のリズムやイントネーションなどに注意して，本文を流暢に音読できるようにしましょう。「スピーキング・トレーナー」を使って，自分の発言を後から確認したり，発話の流暢さ（1分あたりの発話語数：words per minute）を算出することができます。発話の流暢さは80〜110wpm を目指しましょう。

Reading

- ●大学入学共通テストなどの形式に対応した，本文の内容理解問題です。

Vocabulary & Grammar

- ●英検®やGTEC®の形式に対応した，本文中の単語，表現，文法事項についての問題です。

Listening

- ●本文内容やテーマに関連した英文の聞き取り問題です。大学入学共通テストの形式に対応しています。
- ●💿は別売の音声CDのトラック番号を示します。二次元コードを読み取って，音声をPCやスマートフォンなどから聞くこともできます。

Interaction

- ●本文内容やテーマに関連した会話などを聞いて，最後に投げかけられた質問に対して自分の考えなどを応答し，やり取りを完成させる発話問題です。

Production

- ●本文を読んだ感想や，自分の考えや意見などを話したり書いたりして伝える問題です。

◆「知識・技能」や「思考力・判断力・表現力」を養成することを意識し，設問ごとに主に対応する観点を示しました。
◆ライティング，スピーキング問題を自分で採点できるようにしています。
　別冊『解答・解説集』の「ルーブリック評価表」（ある観点における学習の到達度を判断する基準）を用いて，自分の記述内容や発言内容を採点できます。

CONTENTS

CAN-DO List

知識・技能

□語・連語・慣用表現について理解を深め，これらを適切に活用することができる。
□強弱のリズム・イントネーションを理解して音読することができる。

Unit 2

□前の文・節・句全体を先行詞とする関係代名詞 which や，語・連語・慣用表現について理解を深め，これらを適切に活用することができる。
□音の変化を理解して音読することができる。

□文修飾副詞や，語・連語・慣用表現について理解を深め，これらを適切に活用することができる。
□音の変化を理解して音読することができる。

□名詞構文や，語・連語・慣用表現について理解を深め，これらを適切に活用することができる。
□音の変化を理解して音読することができる。

□分詞構文や，語・連語・慣用表現について理解を深め，これらを適切に活用することができる。
□音の変化を理解して音読することができる。

□比較の対象の省略や，語・連語・慣用表現について理解を深め，これらを適切に活用することができる。
□音の変化を理解して音読することができる。

Unit 3

□語・連語・慣用表現について理解を深め，これらを適切に活用することができる。
□シャドーイングをすることができる。

□語・連語・慣用表現について理解を深め，これらを適切に活用することができる。
□シャドーイングをすることができる。

□語・連語・慣用表現について理解を深め，これらを適切に活用することができる。
□シャドーイングをすることができる。

□語・連語・慣用表現について理解を深め，これらを適切に活用することができる。
□シャドーイングをすることができる。

□語・連語・慣用表現について理解を深め，これらを適切に活用することができる。
□シャドーイングをすることができる。

思考力・判断力・表現力

- [ ] 💬 本文内容について的確に理解し，その内容を整理することができる。
- [ ] 🎧 本文内容に関する短い英文を聞いて，必要な情報を把握することができる。
- [ ] 💬 本文に関連するテーマについて，適切に情報や考えを伝え合うことができる。
- [ ] 🗣 本文に関連するテーマについて，自分の考えを話して伝えることができる。
- [ ] ✍ 本文に関連するテーマについて，自分の考えを書いて伝えることができる。

- [ ] 💬 三代達也さんの活動について的確に理解し，その内容を整理することができる。
- [ ] 🎧 事故やバリアフリーに関する短い英文を聞いて，必要な情報を把握することができる。
- [ ] 💬 バリアフリーな社会への取り組みについて，適切に情報や考えを伝え合うことができる。
- [ ] 🗣 困難を乗り越えた経験について，自分の考えを話して伝えることができる。
- [ ] ✍ メンターになってほしい人物や旅行について，自分の考えを書いて伝えることができる。

- [ ] 💬 小田兼利さんの活動について的確に理解し，その内容を整理することができる。
- [ ] 🎧 災害や水問題に関する短い英文を聞いて，必要な情報を把握することができる。
- [ ] 💬 水問題について，適切に情報や考えを伝え合うことができる。
- [ ] 🗣 海外で働くことについて，自分の考えを話して伝えることができる。
- [ ] ✍ 海外で働くことについて，自分の考えを書いて伝えることができる。

- [ ] 💬 『サザエさん』や長谷川町子さんについて的確に理解し，その内容を整理することができる。
- [ ] 🎧 人物の紹介や『サザエさん』に関する短い英文を聞いて，必要な情報を把握することができる。
- [ ] 💬 自分らしく生きることについて，適切に情報や考えを伝え合うことができる。
- [ ] 🗣 ものごとの考え方について，自分の考えを話して伝えることができる。
- [ ] ✍ 家族について，自分の考えを書いて伝えることができる。

- [ ] 💬 ガーナの電子ごみ問題に対する取り組みについて的確に理解し，その内容を整理することができる。
- [ ] 🎧 ガーナやごみ問題に関する短い英文を聞いて，必要な情報を把握することができる。
- [ ] 💬 ガーナや労働問題について，適切に情報や考えを伝え合うことができる。
- [ ] 🗣 クラウドファンディングについて，自分の考えを話して伝えることができる。
- [ ] ✍ ごみ問題やリサイクルについて，自分の考えを書いて伝えることができる。

- [ ] 💬 アイスランドにおける男女平等の取り組みについて的確に理解し，その内容を整理することができる。
- [ ] 🎧 男女平等やストライキに関する短い英文を聞いて，必要な情報を把握することができる。
- [ ] 💬 男女平等について，適切に情報や考えを伝え合うことができる。
- [ ] 🗣 ストライキについて，自分の考えを話して伝えることができる。
- [ ] ✍ 男女平等について，自分の考えを書いて伝えることができる。

- [ ] 💬 魚の乱獲の問題について的確に理解し，その内容を整理することができる。
- [ ] 🎧 海で起こっている問題に関する短い英文を聞いて，必要な情報を把握することができる。
- [ ] 💬 海で起こっている問題について，適切に情報や考えを伝え合うことができる。
- [ ] 🗣 水産資源を守るための取り組みについて，自分の考えを話して伝えることができる。
- [ ] ✍ 水産資源を守るための取り組みや海について，自分の考えを書いて伝えることができる。

- [ ] 💬 大社充さんの活動について的確に理解し，その内容を整理することができる。
- [ ] 🎧 スポーツや戦争や平和に関する短い英文を聞いて，必要な情報を把握することができる。
- [ ] 💬 日常生活について，適切に情報や考えを伝え合うことができる。
- [ ] 🗣 スポーツや平和のための取り組みについて，自分の考えを話して伝えることができる。
- [ ] ✍ 戦争について，自分の考えを書いて伝えることができる。

- [ ] 💬 中村哲医師の活動について的確に理解し，その内容を整理することができる。
- [ ] 🎧 中東や音楽に関する短い英文を聞いて，必要な情報を把握することができる。
- [ ] 💬 干ばつや運河について，適切に情報や考えを伝え合うことができる。
- [ ] 🗣 公共事業や音楽について，自分の考えを話して伝えることができる。
- [ ] ✍ アフガニスタンやパキスタンやノーベル賞について，自分の考えを書いて伝えることができる。

- [ ] 💬 食に関する問題や課題について的確に理解し，その内容を整理することができる。
- [ ] 🎧 食に関する問題や課題に関する短い英文を聞いて，必要な情報を把握することができる。
- [ ] 💬 食料廃棄やフードテックについて，適切に情報や考えを伝え合うことができる。
- [ ] 🗣 フードテックについて，自分の考えを話して伝えることができる。
- [ ] ✍ フードテックや農業について，自分の考えを書いて伝えることができる。

- [ ] 💬 SDGsに関連した取り組みについて的確に理解し，その内容を整理することができる。
- [ ] 🎧 SDGsに関連した取り組みに関する短い英文を聞いて，必要な情報を把握することができる。
- [ ] 💬 教育機関やエネルギーについて，適切に情報や考えを伝え合うことができる。
- [ ] 🗣 SDGsを達成するための取り組みについて，自分の考えを話して伝えることができる。
- [ ] ✍ SDGsを達成するための取り組みについて，自分の考えを書いて伝えることができる。

Naomi Watanabe is one of the most **influential** stars / on social media. // Now / she is recognized / as an international fashion **icon** / and followed / by about 10 million fans. // She started her career / as a comedian / in 2007. // She became popular / for her **exaggerated imitations** / of Beyoncé and Lady Gaga. // In 2019, /
5 she moved to New York / to improve her career. //

Foreign media **praise** Naomi / for her style / in the fields of entertainment and fashion. // Once / she said / in an interview, / "I want people / to treasure who they are / — that's how I **gained** confidence. // I want to tell them / to love themselves." //

(101 words)

Practice 1 スラッシュ位置で文を区切って読んでみよう ☐
Practice 2 英語の強弱のリズムに注意して読んでみよう ☐
TRY! 1分15秒以内に本文全体を音読しよう ☐

📖 **Reading** 本文の内容を読んで理解しよう【知識・技能】【思考力・判断力・表現力】 　(共通テスト)

Make the correct choice to complete each sentence. （各5点）

(1) Naomi changed her place to live and work because ☐.
　① Beyoncé and Lady Gaga advised her to come to New York
　② many influential stars lived in New York
　③ she became an international fashion icon
　④ she wanted to make her career better

(2) ☐ respected in the foreign media.
　① Naomi's exaggerated imitations are
　② Naomi's fashion and activities as a comedian are
　③ Naomi's original style as a fashion designer is
　④ Naomi's own idea to treasure who we are is

(3) One of Naomi's beliefs is that ☐.
　① about 10 million fans follow her on social media
　② her exaggerated imitations have made her popular
　③ she is an international fashion icon
　④ you should value your own identity

Vocabulary & Grammar　重要表現や文法事項について理解しよう【知識】　英検® GTEC®

Make the correct choice to complete each sentence.　（各3点）

(1) My older brother said that the only way to (　　　) confidence is to practice over and over again.

　① amuse　　　　　② contain　　　　　③ gain　　　　　④ organize

(2) *A:* Look!　That is a beautiful flower.

　B: Oh, yeah.　But it seems that it is an (　　　) flower.

　① imagination　　② imitation　　　③ incredible　　　④ intention

(3) Our teacher (　　　) Tom's effort in the class so his face turned red.

　① pleased　　　　② praised　　　　③ promoted　　　④ pronounced

(4) Who do you think was one of the most (　　　) leaders in the 20th century?

　① enormous　　　② expensive　　　③ infectious　　　④ influential

(5) I asked my father (　　　) me up at the station.

　① being picked　　② picked　　　　③ picking　　　　④ to pick

🎧 Listening　英文を聞いて理解しよう【知識・技能】【思考力・判断力・表現力】　共通テスト 💿 2

Listen to the English and make the best choice to match the content.　（4点）

　① The speaker talks about the guest's career and where she comes from.

　② The speaker introduces the guest who has a lot of followers.

　③ The speaker asks the guest to have an interview.

💬 Interaction　英文を聞いて会話を続けよう【知識・技能】【思考力・判断力・表現力】　スピーキング・トレーナー

Listen to the English and respond to the last remark.　（7点）

　〔メモ　　　　　　　　　　　　　　　　　　　　　　　　　　　　　　　　〕

🎤 **Hints**
　have a positive thinking (前向きな考え方をする)，believe I can do it (自分はできると信じる)

😀 Production (Speaking)　自分の考えを話して伝えよう【思考力・判断力・表現力】　スピーキング・トレーナー

Answer the following question.　（9点）

Do you want to live in a foreign country?　Why?

　〔メモ　　　　　　　　　　　　　　　　　　　　　　　　　　　　　　　　〕

🎤 **Hints**
　今，または将来，海外に住みたいかどうかを理由をつけて話してみましょう。

You may know / that some animals / — koalas, kangaroos and wombats / — are **native** to Australia. // But, / how about **quokkas**? // Thanks to their round cheeks and cute smiles, / they are called "the happiest animals on earth." //

Quokkas mainly live / on Rottnest Island / in the **southwest** / of the Australian
5 **mainland**. // The name "Rottnest" / comes from the Dutch **phrase** / for "rat's nest." // When they were first discovered / by Dutch **explorers** / in the 17th century, / they were mistaken / for **giant** rats. //

Quokkas are such friendly **creatures** / that they **approach** tourists / for food. // However, / they are **designated** / as an **endangered species**, / so you are not
10 allowed / to touch or feed them. // But don't be **disappointed**. // Just looking at their smiles / will make you happy. //

(118 words)

🔊)) **音読しよう** 📖 ～～～～～～～～～～～～～～～ スピーキング・トレーナー

Practice 1 スラッシュ位置で文を区切って読んでみよう ☐
Practice 2 英語の強弱のリズムに注意して読んでみよう ☐
TRY! 1分25秒以内に本文全体を音読しよう ☐

📖 Reading 本文の内容を読んで理解しよう【知識・技能】【思考力・判断力・表現力】 共通テスト GTEC®

Make the correct choice to complete each sentence or answer each question. （各5点[(3)は完答]）

(1) Quokkas are called "the happiest animals on earth" because ___.
　① their appearance is similar to kangaroos
　② their habitat is where many animals can be found
　③ they bring good luck to those who meet them
　④ they have round cheeks and their smiles are adorable

(2) What does "disappointed" mean in line 10? ___
　① depressed　　　② impatient　　　③ mad　　　④ pleased

(3) Which of the following are true? (Choose two options. The order does not matter.)
　___ ・ ___
　① Dutch explorers discovered giant rats and quokkas in the 17th century.
　② European explorers found quokkas in the 17th century.
　③ Quokkas are the most well-known Australian animals in Japan.
　④ Quokkas are very friendly animals, so they get close to tourists.
　⑤ Quokkas live on Rottnest Island in the northwest of the Australian mainland.

Vocabulary & Grammar　重要表現や文法事項について理解しよう【知識】　英検® GTEC®

Make the correct choice to complete each sentence.　（各3点）

(1)　Species in danger of extinction are called "(　　　) animals."

　　① effective　　　② endangered　　　③ entire　　　④ expected

(2)　This tree is (　　　) to Africa and is said to be rarely found in any other places.

　　① base　　　② from　　　③ native　　　④ original

(3)　*Kappa* is an imaginary (　　　) and there are a lot of stories about it in Japan.

　　① create　　　② creative　　　③ creator　　　④ creature

(4)　Naomi Uemura was the first Japanese (　　　) to climb Mt. Everest.

　　① examinee　　　② examiner　　　③ explorer　　　④ exporter

(5)　The story made the children (　　　).

　　① be excited　　　② excited　　　③ excites　　　④ exciting

🎧 Listening　英文を聞いて理解しよう【知識・技能】【思考力・判断力・表現力】　共通テスト　● 3

Listen to the English and make the best choice to match the content.　（4点）

　　① Some Australian animals don't have any special parts of their bodies.

　　② Some Australian animals raise their babies without milk.

　　③ Some Australian animals have a unique style to raise their babies.

💬 Interaction　英文を聞いて会話を続けよう【知識・技能】【思考力・判断力・表現力】　スピーキング・トレーナー

Listen to the English and respond to the last remark.　（7点）

〔メモ　　　　　　　　　　　　　　　　　　　　　　　　　　　　　　　　　　　　〕

🌡 **Hints**

conservation (保護)，wildlife (野生生物)，ecosystem (生態系)，observe (…を観察する)，donate (…を寄付する)

✍ Production (Writing)　自分の考えを書いて伝えよう【思考力・判断力・表現力】

Write your answer to the following question.　（9点）

Give an example of an endangered animal and explain the reason why it is endangered.

🌡 **Hints**

polar bear (ホッキョクグマ)，rhino (サイ)，giant panda (ジャイアントパンダ)，fur (毛皮)，horn (ツノ)

Do you know of Taro Okamoto, / who was one of the most famous Japanese artists? // As a painter, **sculptor** and writer, / he challenged traditional Japanese values. //

As a producer of **Expo** '70, / Okamoto created *the Tower of the Sun*, / a
5 monument / **overflowing** with **primitive** power. // At that time, / it was **severely criticized** / by some artists / because it didn't seem to **reflect** / the traditional Japanese sense of beauty. // Yet, / such **criticism** didn't **discourage** him / at all. // He was an artist / with a **consistent** attitude / and strong beliefs. // Now / *the Tower of the Sun* is considered / one of his most outstanding works. //

(100 words)

🔊 **音読しよう** 📖 　　　　　　　　　　　　　　　　スピーキング・トレーナー

Practice 1 スラッシュ位置で文を区切って読んでみよう ☐
Practice 2 英語の強弱のリズムに注意して読んでみよう ☐
TRY! 1分10秒以内に本文全体を音読しよう ☐

📖 **Reading** 本文の内容を読んで理解しよう【知識・技能】【思考力・判断力・表現力】　共通テスト GTEC®

Make the correct choice to complete each sentence or answer each question. （各5点）

(1) What does "primitive" mean in line 5? ☐
　① cheerful　　　　② complex　　　　③ early　　　　④ tough

(2) Which of the following is true? ☐
　① People think *the Tower of the Sun* is a traditional Japanese monument.
　② People think *the Tower of the Sun* is one of Taro's greatest artworks.
　③ *The Tower of the Sun* was destroyed soon after Expo '70 ended.
　④ *The Tower of the Sun* was made for Expo '70 and welcomed in the world.

(3) When *the Tower of the Sun* was criticized, Taro ☐.
　① insisted that it had primitive power to reflect the traditional Japanese sense of beauty
　② reworked it to express the traditional Japanese sense of beauty
　③ tried to be consistent, but finally changed his mind
　④ was not disappointed at all

🔊 英語の強弱のリズムを理解して音読することができる。　📖 岡本太郎さんに関する英文を読んで概要や要点をとらえることができる。

✏️ 文脈を理解して適切な語句を用いて英文を完成することができる。　🎧 平易な英語で話される短い英文を聞いて必要な情報を聞き取ることができる。

🗣️ 万国博覧会について簡単な語句を用いて情報や考えを伝えることができる。　✍️ 好きな芸術作品について簡単な語句を用いて考えを表現することができる。

🏷️ Vocabulary & Grammar　重要表現や文法事項について理解しよう【知識】　英検® GTEC®

Make the correct choice to complete each sentence.　（各 3 点）

(1) It is said that people ate some kinds of nuts during (　　　) times.
　　① practical　　　　② primitive　　　　③ private　　　　④ promising

(2) Finally, our opinion was (　　　) in the government policy.
　　① reflected　　　　② related　　　　③ replaced　　　　④ returned

(3) The terrible test results (　　　) Tom.
　　① disagreed　　　　② disappeared　　　　③ discouraged　　　　④ discovered

(4) What he said about the accident was (　　　) with some reports.
　　① consistent　　　　② likely　　　　③ resembled　　　　④ similar

(5) I read *Alice's Adventures in Wonderland*, (　　　) was written by Lewis Carroll.
　　① that　　　　② which　　　　③ who　　　　④ whose

🎧 Listening　英文を聞いて理解しよう【知識・技能】【思考力・判断力・表現力】　共通テスト　4

Listen to the English and make the best choice to match the content.　（4 点）

　① The speaker criticizes the new system.

　② The speaker praises the people who are planning to create the new system.

　③ The speaker says the new system has helped protect her personal information.

💬 Interaction　英文を聞いて会話を続けよう【知識・技能】【思考力・判断力・表現力】　スピーキング・トレーナー

Listen to the English and respond to the last remark.　（7 点）

〔メ モ 　　〕

🎧 **Hints**

virtual (仮想の)，avatar (アバター)，exhibition (展示)，latest (最新の)

✍️ Production（Writing）　自分の考えを書いて伝えよう【思考力・判断力・表現力】

Write your answer to the following question.　（9 点）

What famous artwork do you like the best?　Why?

🎧 **Hints**

The Starry Night (星月夜)，Vincent van Gogh (フィンセント・ファン・ゴッホ)

Gitanjali Rao was selected / as *TIME*'s 2020 "Kid of the Year" / at the age of 15. // The Indian-American scientist and **inventor** / uses technology / to solve social and environmental problems. //

For example, / Gitanjali invented an AI-based service / called "Kindly." // It
5 **detects** words / that could be related to **cyberbullying**. // She also created "Tethys," / a device / that can **identify** lead **contamination** / in drinking water. //

Her **mission** doesn't stop there. // Gitanjali has also held **innovative** workshops / on STEM / globally. // With these workshops, / she **intends** to create a global community / of young **innovators** / to **tackle** world problems. // She says, / "It's
10 never too early / to start making a difference. // Every one of us / has the power / to change the world." //

(114 words)

🔊)) 音読しよう 📖 ～～～～～～～ スピーキング・トレーナー

Practice 1 スラッシュ位置で文を区切って読んでみよう ☐
Practice 2 英語の強弱のリズムに注意して読んでみよう ☐
TRY! 1分25秒以内に本文全体を音読しよう ☐

📖 **Reading** 本文の内容を読んで理解しよう【知識・技能】【思考力・判断力・表現力】 共通テスト GTEC®

Make the correct choice to complete each sentence or answer each question. （各5点[(1)は完答]）

(1) Which of the following are true? (Choose two options. The order does not matter.) ☐ · ☐

① Gitanjali believes it takes a lot of time to do something different.
② Gitanjali created an AI-based service to prevent cyberbullying.
③ Gitanjali got *TIME*'s "Kid of the Year" when she was fifteen.
④ "Tethys" can automatically remove lead contamination from drinking water.
⑤ *TIME*'s "Kid of the Year" is a selection of outstanding 15-year-olds from around the world.

(2) What does "contamination" mean in line 6? ☐
① impression ② innovation ③ pollution ④ relation

(3) Gitanjali ☐.
① expects that young scientists need more time to change the world
② has already accomplished all of her missions
③ is sure that people can change the world
④ thinks that it's too late to solve global problems

🎴 Vocabulary & Grammar 重要表現や文法事項について理解しよう【知識】 (英検®)(GTEC®)

Make the correct choice to complete each sentence. （各3点）

(1) I didn't (　　　) to cause such a terrible accident.

① include　　　② insist　　　③ intend　　　④ invade

(2) Mr. Suzuki was (　　　) as Most Valuable Player (MVP) last year.

① described　　② related　　③ selected　　④ used

(3) Some police officers have a specific skill to (　　　) poison.

① ideal　　　② identical　　③ identify　　④ identity

(4) My grandfather (　　　) health challenges to overcome his illness.

① tackled　　② traded　　③ translated　　④ transported

(5) These clothes are (　　　) expensive for me to buy.

① as　　　② enough　　　③ so　　　④ too

🎧 Listening 英文を聞いて理解しよう【知識・技能】【思考力・判断力・表現力】 (共通テスト) 💿 5

Listen to the English and make the best choice to match the content. （4点）

① An exchange student is talking about the next contest.

② Innovative ideas are expected for the next contest.

③ In the next contest, a very expensive item will be exhibited.

💬 Interaction 英文を聞いて会話を続けよう【知識・技能】【思考力・判断力・表現力】 スピーキング・トレーナー

Listen to the English and respond to the remarks. （7点）

〔メモ　　　　　　　　　　　　　　　　　　　　　　　　　　　　　　　〕

🖐Hints

effort (努力), patient (忍耐強い), seriously (まじめに), achieve (…を達成する), goal (目標)

💬 Production (Speaking) 自分の考えを話して伝えよう【思考力・判断力・表現力】 スピーキング・トレーナー

Answer the following question. （9点）

If you join an international workshop, what subjects would you like to discuss?

〔メモ　　　　　　　　　　　　　　　　　　　　　　　　　　　　　　　〕

🖐Hints

history (歴史), economics (経済), mathematics (数学), energy (エネルギー)

Look at these pictures. // They all have the **"golden ratio"** / in them. // The golden ratio is a **mathematical** ratio / of 1:1.618. //

It is said / that many famous **architectural** works, / artworks / and other objects / have been **composed** / with this ratio. // For example, / the **Pyramids**
5 of Giza in Egypt, / the Parthenon in Athens, / and Kinkakuji Temple in Kyoto / are among them. //

Why are people attracted / to these structures? // It may be / because the golden ratio is a kind of law / and order of nature. // We can also find the golden ratio / in beautiful objects / in nature, / such as flowers, / **ferns** / and **seashells**. //
10 When we see objects / with this ratio, / we **instinctively** feel / that they are **well-balanced**, / **pleasing** / and beautiful. //

(117 words)

音読しよう   スピーキング・トレーナー

Practice 1 スラッシュ位置で文を区切って読んでみよう ☐
Practice 2 英語の強弱のリズムに注意して読んでみよう ☐
TRY! 1分25秒以内に本文全体を音読しよう ☐

Reading 本文の内容を読んで理解しよう【知識・技能】【思考力・判断力・表現力】   共通テスト GTEC®

Make the correct choice to complete each sentence or answer each question. (各5点)

(1) According to the article, many famous works ☐.
① have been created using the golden ratio
② might have been made of gold
③ were created by architects and mathematicians
④ with the golden ratio can only be seen in Europe

(2) What does "ratio" mean in line 1? ☐
① method   ② process   ③ proportion   ④ texture

(3) One **opinion** from the article is that ☐.
① all objects in nature have the golden ratio
② some flowers, ferns, and seashells have the golden ratio
③ the golden ratio might be set by the rules of nature
④ the Parthenon in Athens was composed with the golden ratio

Vocabulary & Grammar　重要表現や文法事項について理解しよう【知識】　英検® GTEC®

Make the correct choice to complete each sentence. （各3点）

(1) This organization is (　　　) of famous professors from around the world.

① communicated　② composed　③ connected　④ consumed

(2) We need to have a healthy and (　　　) diet every day.

① welfare　② well-balanced　③ well-built　④ well-known

(3) The sound of the bell was extremely (　　　) to me.

① please　② pleased　③ pleasing　④ pleasure

(4) This graph shows the (　　　) of births and deaths.

① addition　② division　③ ratio　④ times

(5) My bike has (　　　) yet so I have to go to school on foot this morning.

① been fixed　② been fixing　③ not been fixed　④ not fixed

🎧 Listening　英文を聞いて理解しよう【知識・技能】【思考力・判断力・表現力】　共通テスト　💿6

Listen to the English and make the best choice to match the content. （4点）

① A lot of tourists are impressed by Spanish food.

② The large church has not been completed yet.

③ There are many churches under construction in Spain.

💬 Interaction　英文を聞いて会話を続けよう【知識・技能】【思考力・判断力・表現力】　スピーキング・トレーナー

Listen to the English and respond to the last remark. （7点）

〔メ モ　　　　　　　　　　　　　　　　　　　　　　　　　　　　　　　　〕

🎸 **Hints**

business card (名刺)，logo ((商標・社名などの)ロゴ)，credit card (クレジットカード)，postcard (はがき)

😀 Production（Speaking）　自分の考えを話して伝えよう【思考力・判断力・表現力】　スピーキング・トレーナー

Answer the following question. （9点）

What is the most impressive building or artwork you have ever seen?

〔メ モ　　　　　　　　　　　　　　　　　　　　　　　　　　　　　　　　〕

🎸 **Hints**

思いつかない場合は，見てみたい建造物や芸術作品について話しましょう。

教科書 p. 16-17 　　／ 50

　　Have you ever heard / of **"ethical consumption"**? // It means / to choose products or services / in **consideration** of the environment, / human rights, / or animal welfare. //

　　How can we become ethical **consumers**? // For example, / we can choose
5　ethical products / such as fair-trade, eco-friendly or recycled products. // When shopping, / it is important / to consider / how the products were produced / before buying them. // Choosing ethical products / can help to improve our society. //

　　We can also help to save the environment / by **installing** solar panels / or
10　choosing **electric appliances** / with low power consumption. // The time is just around the corner / when it will be normal / to live as an ethical consumer. //

(106 words)

音読しよう 📖 ～～～～～～～～～～　スピーキング・トレーナー

Practice 1 スラッシュ位置で文を区切って読んでみよう ☐
Practice 2 英語の強弱のリズムに注意して読んでみよう ☐
TRY! 1分15秒以内に本文全体を音読しよう ☐

Reading 本文の内容を読んで理解しよう【知識・技能】【思考力・判断力・表現力】 　共通テスト GTEC®

Make the correct choice to complete each sentence or answer each question. (各5点)

(1) To become an ethical consumer, you should **not** choose ☐.
　① a car which has a low impact on the environment
　② cats or dogs which are treated illegally at pet shops
　③ coffee imported from a developing country as a fair-trade product
　④ paper made from household waste or waste paper

(2) What does "welfare" mean in line 3? ☐
　① well-balanced　　② well-being　　③ well-done　　④ well-known

(3) According to the article, ☐.
　① people will pay more attention to ethical consumption in the near future
　② the installation of solar panels has increased electricity consumption
　③ the number of ethical consumers is decreasing rapidly
　④ there is no way to know whether a product is ethical or not before you buy it

📇 Vocabulary & Grammar　重要表現や文法事項について理解しよう【知識】　(英検®) (GTEC®)

Make the correct choice to complete each sentence. （各3点）

(1) This event must be scheduled in (　　　　) of the season in Japan.
　① conservation　　② consideration　　③ construction　　④ contribution

(2) I (　　　　) a new game application on my computer.
　① entered　　② fixed　　③ installed　　④ instructed

(3) Ted will purchase some (　　　　) to live on his own this April.
　① admissions　　② appearances　　③ appliances　　④ awards

(4) Choosing (　　　　) vehicles is one of the most eco-friendly solutions.
　① electric　　② electricity　　③ electronic　　④ energy

(5) The day will soon come (　　　　) we can drive flying cars.
　① that　　② what　　③ when　　④ which

🎧 Listening　英文を聞いて理解しよう【知識・技能】【思考力・判断力・表現力】　(共通テスト) 💿7

Listen to the English and make the best choice to match the content. （4点）

　① Delicious seafood from the disaster-affected areas can be purchased online.

　② If you buy the seafood, you can support specific regions.

　③ While the speaker was enjoying a delicious meal, a terrible disaster happened.

💬 Interaction　英文を聞いて会話を続けよう【知識・技能】【思考力・判断力・表現力】　スピーキング・トレーナー

Listen to the English and respond to the last remark. （7点）

〔メモ　　　　　　　　　　　　　　　　　　　　　　　　　　　　　　　　　　　　　　〕

🎤 **Hints**
　エシカルな消費者となるために何を考慮すべきかを考えよう。

✒️ Production (Writing)　自分の考えを書いて伝えよう【思考力・判断力・表現力】

Write your answer to the following question. （9点）

What do you think are the advantages of buying locally produced goods?

🎤 **Hints**
　local production for local consumption（地産地消）, producer（生産者）, fresh（新鮮な）, transportation（輸送）

Do you know / there are some jungle schools / for **orangutans**? // These unique schools / to protect them / are located / in a jungle / in Borneo, / Indonesia. //

The orangutans / at these schools / have been left **orphans**. // They can't
5 live / in the real **wilderness** / without first being taught **survival** skills / by humans. // That's why they are learning / how to build **sturdy** nests, / how to **crack coconuts**, / and even how to climb trees. //

Orangutans are losing their homes / because their rainforest habitat / is being destroyed / due to human activities / such as plantation development / and
10 **illegal** deforestation. // As a result, / they are in danger of extinction. // What do you think / about the **selfishness** / of human beings? //

(110 words)

Practice 1 スラッシュ位置で文を区切って読んでみよう ☐
Practice 2 英語の強弱のリズムに注意して読んでみよう ☐
TRY! 1分20秒以内に本文全体を音読しよう ☐

Reading 本文の内容を読んで理解しよう【知識・技能】【思考力・判断力・表現力】 (共通テスト)

Make the correct choice to complete each sentence or answer each question. （各5点）

(1) Which of the following is true about jungle schools in Borneo? [____]
　① Humans are taught how to climb trees by orangutans.
　② Humans are taught how to crack coconuts by orangutans.
　③ Orangutans teach humans how to cut down trees.
　④ Orangutans are taught how to make a safe place to live in by humans.

(2) Orangutans have lost their habitat because [____].
　① people have overhunted them for various experiments
　② people have tried to expand their farmlands
　③ they didn't know the skills necessary to survive in the wild
　④ they picked too many coconuts for food

(3) One **opinion** from the article is that [____].
　① in Indonesia, there are schools where humans teach orangutans various things
　② orangutans without parents cannot survive in the jungle unless they learn how to live
　③ the orangutans in Borneo are endangered because of humans
　④ we should consider human selfishness

🔊 英語の強弱のリズムを理解して音読することができる。 📖 オランウータンの学校に関する英文を読んで概要や要点をとらえることができる。

文脈を理解して適切な語句を用いて英文を完成することができる。 🎧 平易な英語で話される短い英文を聞いて必要な情報を聞き取ることができる。

動物を飼うことについて簡単な語句を用いて情報や考えを伝えることができる。 ✍ 野生動物との共生について簡単な語句を用いて考えを表現することができる。

🗂 Vocabulary & Grammar　重要表現や文法事項について理解しよう【知識】　英検® GTEC®

Make the correct choice to complete each sentence. （各3点）

(1) Seattle is (　　　) in the western part of the United States.

① existed　　　② limited　　　③ located　　　④ set

(2) It is (　　　) to take oysters from this beach.

① empty　　　② illegal　　　③ initial　　　④ positive

(3) This table, which my grandmother used for a long time, is old but (　　　).

① resistant　　　② severe　　　③ sturdy　　　④ tight

(4) It's amazing that you can (　　　) an egg with one hand.

① click　　　② crack　　　③ knock　　　④ strike

(5) The closet in this room has not (　　　) for a long time.

① been opened　　　② been opening　　　③ opened　　　④ opening

🎧 Listening　英文を聞いて理解しよう【知識・技能】【思考力・判断力・表現力】　共通テスト　💿 8

Listen to the English and make the best choice to match the content. （4点）

① The speaker decided to live with the puppies.

② The speaker did volunteering at an animal shelter.

③ The speaker was pleased that the puppies had new families.

💬 Interaction　英文を聞いて会話を続けよう【知識・技能】【思考力・判断力・表現力】　スピーキング・トレーナー

Listen to the English and respond to the last remark. （7点）

〔メモ　　〕

🎧 Hints

feed (…にえさをやる)，take a dog for a walk (犬を散歩に連れて行く)，life-change (生活の変化)

✍ Production（Writing）　自分の考えを書いて伝えよう【思考力・判断力・表現力】

Write your answer to the following question. （9点）

Sometimes wild animals come to towns and damage crops. How can we live in harmony with them?

🔊 Hints

野生動物と共存するためにはどうしたらよいか考えてみよう。

"One Team" was Japan's **slogan** / for the 2019 Rugby World Cup. // Sixteen of Japan's 31 players / were born / in other nations. // The **unity** / shown by these players / of different backgrounds / surely moved the public. //

Captain Michael Leitch, / a New Zealand-born Japanese, / created various
5 opportunities / for the foreign-born players / to learn about Japan. // For example, / he held quiz events / to teach them / about the country's history. // Michael said, / "If they learn more / about Japan, / we can become even more **united** / as one team." //

The team can be seen / as a mirror / of today's Japan. // Many people / from
10 **diverse** backgrounds / are gradually becoming part of Japanese society. // As a result, / the **diversity** / they bring / can help Japan build a new era. //

(119 words)

音読しよう

Practice 1 スラッシュ位置で文を区切って読んでみよう ☐
Practice 2 英語の強弱のリズムに注意して読んでみよう ☐
TRY! 1分25秒以内に本文全体を音読しよう ☐

Reading 本文の内容を読んで理解しよう【知識・技能】【思考力・判断力・表現力】 (共通テスト)

Make the correct choice to complete each sentence or answer each question. (各5点)

(1) Which of the following is true about "One Team"? ☐
 ① It is a slogan that captain Michael Leitch came up with.
 ② It is a slogan used by the Japanese national rugby team every year.
 ③ It means the Japanese national rugby team consists of only one nationality.
 ④ It means that players of different backgrounds should cooperate with each other.

(2) Michael Leitch ☐.
 ① gave his teammates many opportunities to learn about Japanese history
 ② is a New Zealander born and raised in Japan
 ③ often quizzed his teammates about New Zealand
 ④ was one of sixteen players on the Japanese national rugby team in 2019

(3) One **opinion** from the article is that ☐.
 ① Michael Leitch tried to let his teammates know a lot about Japan
 ② the team diversity can help Japan build a terrible era
 ③ the Japanese national rugby team was composed of players of various nationalities
 ④ a new era may come to Japan thanks to the diversity

Goals

🔊 英語の強弱のリズムを理解して音読することができる。　📖 ラグビー日本代表チームに関する英文を読んで概要や要点をとらえることができる。
📝 文脈を理解して適切な語句を用いて英文を完成することができる。　🎧 平易な英語で話される短い英文を聞いて必要な情報を聞き取ることができる。
💬 ニュージーランドについて簡単な語句を用いて情報や考えを伝えることができる。　🗨 チーム内での役割について簡単な語句を用いて考えを表現することができる。

🔊 Vocabulary & Grammar　重要表現や文法事項について理解しよう【知識】　英検® GTEC®

Make the correct choice to complete each sentence.　(各3点)

(1) Some political (　　　　) have been shown on the signboard.

　① scales　　　　② seeds　　　　③ slogans　　　　④ sloths

(2) He is full of curiosity and has (　　　　) interests.

　① all　　　　② diverse　　　　③ every　　　　④ variety

(3) I was deeply (　　　　) by my teacher's words.

　① carried　　　　② carrying　　　　③ moved　　　　④ moving

(4) Now it's time for us to (　　　　) our efforts to make this event a success.

　① explode　　　　② involve　　　　③ switch　　　　④ unite

(5) Sushi is a traditional Japanese food (　　　　) by people around the world.

　① developed　　　　② loved　　　　③ used　　　　④ spoken

🎧 Listening　英文を聞いて理解しよう【知識・技能】【思考力・判断力・表現力】　共通テスト　💿 9

Listen to the English and make the best choice to match the content.　(4点)

　① People of different nationalities attended the meeting.

　② The speaker is making a speech about the importance of diversity.

　③ The speaker is wondering which is most important: race, nationality, or identity.

💬 Interaction　英文を聞いて会話を続けよう【知識・技能】【思考力・判断力・表現力】　スピーキング・トレーナー

Listen to the English and respond to the last remark.　(7点)

〔メモ　　　　　　　　　　　　　　　　　　　　　　　　　　　　　　　　　〕

🎧 **Hints**
cricket (クリケット), kiwi (キーウィ (ニュージーランドに生息する鳥)), kiwi fruit (キウイフルーツ), sheep (羊)

🗨 Production (Speaking)　自分の考えを話して伝えよう【思考力・判断力・表現力】　スピーキング・トレーナー

Answer the following question.　(9点)

If you were a reserve player on a soccer team, what could you do to contribute to the team?

〔メモ　　　　　　　　　　　　　　　　　　　　　　　　　　　　　　　　　〕

🎧 **Hints**
チームのために何ができるか，補欠選手の立場で考えてみよう。

Everyone hopes to be healthy / and live a long life. // Will it ever be possible / for humans / to gain **immortality**, / then? //

Researchers hold different views / on this question. // Some **argue** / that **everlasting** life will be possible, / in the future, / while others think / it's

5 **unlikely**. // However, / many of them seem to agree / that we can delay aging. // One of the key **factors** / is to **activate** our "**longevity** genes." // This could be made possible, / for example, / by reducing our **calorie intake**. // The activated genes / could help damaged **cells recover**. // Moreover, / they might also prevent some serious diseases. //

10 **Extending** our life **span** / may lead to great changes / in our society. // People might **retire** / at the age of 85, / or **centenarian** athletes might even take part in the Olympics! //

(125 words)

🗣️)) 【音読しよう】📖   〔スピーキング・トレーナー〕

Practice 1 スラッシュ位置で文を区切って読んでみよう ☐
Practice 2 英語の強弱のリズムに注意して読んでみよう ☐
TRY! 1分30秒以内に本文全体を音読しよう ☐

📖 **Reading** 本文の内容を読んで理解しよう【知識・技能】【思考力・判断力・表現力】   〔共通テスト〕〔GTEC®〕

Make the correct choice to complete each sentence or answer each question. (各5点)

(1) What does "prevent" mean in line 9? ☐
　① avoid   ② devote   ③ prepare   ④ struggle

(2) The likely effective way to delay aging is to ☐.
　① consume more calories than before
　② make specific genes work well
　③ prevent some serious diseases
　④ recover damaged cells

(3) One **fact** from the article is that ☐.
　① activating the "longevity genes" will help you live longer
　② extending our life span may help our society change
　③ researchers have different opinions about immortality
　④ the activated genes make our body young

🏷 Vocabulary & Grammar 重要表現や文法事項について理解しよう【知識】 (英検®) (GTEC®)

Make the correct choice to complete each sentence. （各3点）

(1) He (   ) that the government should take action regarding the recent price increases.

　① appeared 　　　② argued 　　　③ arrested 　　　④ avoided

(2) My uncle will (   ) from his company next month and start his own business.

　① rely 　　　② repair 　　　③ respond 　　　④ retire

(3) Kate is (   ) from her injury.

　① fixing 　　　② placing 　　　③ recovering 　　　④ returning

(4) Because we have not yet finished the task, we all hope that the deadline will be (   ).

　① excused 　　　② exported 　　　③ exposed 　　　④ extended

(5) He seems to (   ) a lot of money from his friends in the past.

　① be borrowed 　　　② borrow 　　　③ have been borrowed 　④ have borrowed

🎧 Listening 英文を聞いて理解しよう【知識・技能】【思考力・判断力・表現力】 (共通テスト) 🔟

Listen to the English and make the best choice to match the content. （4点）

　① People will be able to get a new medicine in the future.

　② The speaker does not need advanced technology.

　③ The speaker made a new medicine for delaying aging.

💬 Interaction 英文を聞いて会話を続けよう【知識・技能】【思考力・判断力・表現力】 (スピーキング・トレーナー)

Listen to the English and respond to the last remark. （7点）

　〔メ　モ　　　　　　　　　　　　　　　　　　　　　　　　　　　　　　　　　　　〕

🎵 **Hints**
　play shogi (将棋をする)，play gate ball (ゲートボールをする)，have a well-balanced diet (バランスのよい食事をとる)

😀 Production (Speaking) 自分の考えを話して伝えよう【思考力・判断力・表現力】 (スピーキング・トレーナー)

Answer the following question. （9点）

If you were to live longer, would you retire at the age of 85?

　〔メ　モ　　　　　　　　　　　　　　　　　　　　　　　　　　　　　　　　　　　〕

🎵 **Hints**
　自分の老後をイメージして，やりたいことやできることを話してみましょう。

The train came out / of the long **tunnel** / into the snow country. //

This is the opening passage / of the **novel**, / *Snow Country*, / written by Yasunari Kawabata. // This passage / in English / was translated / by Edward George Seidensticker, / an American **scholar** / of Japanese **literature**. //

5　Compared with the original, / how is his translation different? //

The sentence / in the Japanese original / has no **explicit** subject. // On the other hand, / Seidensticker translated the sentence / by using "the train" / as the subject. // Unlike Japanese, / subjects are usually required / in English. //

In addition, / in the English version, / the **scenery** is described **objectively** / with a view / from the sky, / while it is viewed **subjectively** / from inside the train / in the Japanese original. // In this way, / if we compare Japanese novels / with their English translations, / we can **observe** their different ways / of seeing the world. //

(136 words)

🔊 **音読しよう** 📖　　　　　　　　　　　　　　　スピーキング・トレーナー

Practice 1 スラッシュ位置で文を区切って読んでみよう ☐
Practice 2 英語の強弱のリズムに注意して読んでみよう ☐
TRY! 1分40秒以内に本文全体を音読しよう ☐

📖 Reading　本文の内容を読んで理解しよう【知識・技能】【思考力・判断力・表現力】　　共通テスト GTEC®

Make the correct choice to complete each sentence or answer each question. （各5点）

(1) What does "unlike" mean in line 8? ☐
　① call for　　　② different from　　③ look over　　④ similar to

(2) Seidensticker used "the train" in the passage because ☐.
　① English usually requires a clear subject
　② he saw the world differently than Yasunari did
　③ he wanted to describe the scenery subjectively
　④ the subject in the Japanese original was a train

(3) One **opinion** from the article is that ☐.
　① people can find a new way to see the world by reading Japanese novels and their English translations
　② people cannot describe things objectively in Japanese
　③ subjects are usually required in English
　④ the first sentence in the Japanese original of *Snow Country* does not have an explicit subject

🏷 Vocabulary & Grammar　重要表現や文法事項について理解しよう【知識】　英検® GTEC®

Make the correct choice to complete each sentence.　（各3点）

(1) My teacher said, "Don't (　　　) yourself with others."

　① compare　　　　② contact　　　　③ continue　　　　④ convey

(2) I think it is time for you to look at yourself (　　　).

　① approximately　② conveniently　③ eventually　④ objectively

(3) Sally made an (　　　) decision about her career after much thought.

　① explicit　　　　② illegal　　　　③ indirect　　　　④ instant

(4) We enjoyed the beautiful (　　　) during our trip to Hokkaido.

　① scale　　　　　② scenery　　　　③ scissors　　　　④ scream

(5) (　　　) very tired yesterday, I didn't want to take my dog for a walk.

　① Being felt　　　② Feel　　　　③ Feeling　　　　④ Felt

🎧 Listening　英文を聞いて理解しよう【知識・技能】【思考力・判断力・表現力】　共通テスト　💿11

Listen to the English and make the best choice to match the content.　（4点）

　① One famous Japanese novelist is introduced.

　② Yasunari Kawabata was awarded the Nobel Peace Prize.

　③ Yasunari Kawabata won the Nobel Prize and expressed his gratitude.

💬 Interaction　英文を聞いて会話を続けよう【知識・技能】【思考力・判断力・表現力】　スピーキング・トレーナー

Listen to the English and respond to the remarks.　（7点）

〔メ モ　　　　　　　　　　　　　　　　　　　　　　　　　　　　　　　　〕

🔑 **Hints**

英語に限らず，原語で触れてみたいものについて話してみよう。

✍ Production（Writing）　自分の考えを書いて伝えよう【思考力・判断力・表現力】

Write your answer to the following question.　（9点）

What do you think is the biggest difference between Japanese and English?

🔑 **Hints**

pronunciation (発音)，consonant (子音)，article (冠詞)，order (順序)，letter (文字)

Keisuke Honda is a well-known professional soccer player. // In 2010, / Keisuke was in South Africa / to play in the World Cup. // He visited an **orphanage**, / where he saw many **miserable** children. // This experience made him / **aware** of what he could do / to make the world a better place. //

5 Now, / as an **entrepreneur**, / Keisuke is trying hard / to offer people opportunities / to **pursue** their dreams. // First of all, / he established soccer schools / inside and outside Japan. // Next, / he set up funds / with famous and **distinguished** people / all over the world. // As a gifted and **talented** person, / he is **conscious** of his mission / to give people in need / a path to success. //

(110 words)

音読しよう   スピーキング・トレーナー

Practice 1 スラッシュ位置で文を区切って読んでみよう ☐
Practice 2 イントネーションに注意して読んでみよう ☐
TRY! 1分10秒以内に本文全体を音読しよう ☐

Reading 本文の内容を読んで理解しよう【知識・技能】【思考力・判断力・表現力】   共通テスト GTEC®

Make the correct choice to complete each sentence or answer each question. (各5点)

(1) What does "offer" mean in line 5? ☐
   ① approach   ② involve   ③ provide   ④ receive

(2) Which of the following is **not** true? ☐
   ① Keisuke created funds with famous people from all over the world.
   ② Keisuke is trying to give people opportunities to achieve their goals.
   ③ Keisuke established soccer schools in Japan and some companies in South Africa.
   ④ Keisuke realized what he could do after visiting an orphanage in South Africa.

(3) Keisuke thinks that ☐.
   ① gifted and talented people should donate some money to charity
   ② his mission is to make a path to freedom for miserable children
   ③ he must give some gifts to people in need
   ④ he should support people who need help

Vocabulary & Grammar　重要表現や文法事項について理解しよう【知識】　英検® GTEC®

Make the correct choice to complete each sentence.　(各3点)

(1) Most people are (　　　) of the dangers of smoking.

　① aware　　　　② fond　　　　③ independent　　　④ proud

(2) My father often tells me that it is important to (　　　) a definite goal.

　① command　　② pursue　　　③ rid　　　　　④ warn

(3) When Rick was a child, he had a really (　　　) experience which made him quiet.

　① charming　　② excellent　　③ general　　　④ miserable

(4) This statue is one of the most (　　　) works in the museum.

　① detective　　② developing　③ distant　　　④ distinguished

(5) Unfortunately, the cake shop, (　　　) I often buy chocolate cake, was closed today.

　① that　　　　② where　　　③ which　　　　④ whose

Listening　英文を聞いて理解しよう【知識・技能】【思考力・判断力・表現力】　共通テスト 💿12

Listen to the English and make the best choice to match the content.　(4点)

　① The speaker is talking about activities that professional athletes do.

　② The speaker often teaches children as a volunteer.

　③ The speaker says that professional athletes collect donations from their fans.

Interaction　英文を聞いて会話を続けよう【知識・技能】【思考力・判断力・表現力】　スピーキング・トレーナー

Listen to the English and respond to the last remark.　(7点)

〔メ　モ　　　　　　　　　　　　　　　　　　　　　　　　　　　　　　　　　　　〕

🎧 **Hints**

cartoonist (漫画家)，painter (画家)，director ((映画・テレビ番組などの)監督)，YouTuber (ユーチューバー)

Production(Writing)　自分の考えを書いて伝えよう【思考力・判断力・表現力】

Write your answer to the following question.　(9点)

What experience changed you? If you don't have such an experience, what experience do you think would change you?

_____

_____

🎧 **Hints**

traffic accident (交通事故)，earthquake (地震)，live by oneself (一人暮らしをする)，study abroad (海外に留学する)

VR (**virtual** reality) technology has been developing / in the field of entertainment. // The moment we put on head-**mounted** VR **goggles**, / we can **dive** into a virtual world / and become a hero or a **heroine** / in a game. //

In addition to entertainment, / VR technology has been **applied** / to other

5 fields / as well. // First, / this technology is also used / in medical fields. // It is used / by **surgeons** / to **rehearse complex operations**. // Second, / teachers can apply this technology / to their classrooms. // In a geography class, / for example, / students can visit any place / on the **globe** / on a virtual field trip. // Third, / VR-based training is offered / to prepare against natural disasters. //

10 VR technology will surely keep on developing. // We can continue / to expect many surprising benefits / from it. //

(124 words)

音読しよう

Practice 1 スラッシュ位置で文を区切って読んでみよう ☐
Practice 2 イントネーションに注意して読んでみよう ☐
TRY! 1分20秒以内に本文全体を音読しよう ☐

スピーキング・トレーナー

Reading 本文の内容を読んで理解しよう【知識・技能】【思考力・判断力・表現力】   共通テスト

Make the correct choice to complete each sentence or answer each question. (各5点)

(1) As soon as we put on a VR device, ☐.

① a virtual game gives us a special experience in an unreal world

② a virtual world gives us the ability to develop technology

③ we can dive into a real world

④ we can play a game with a hero or a heroine in the game

(2) Which of the following fields is **not** mentioned in the passage? ☐

① Agriculture.   ② Education.

③ Entertainment.   ④ Disaster prevention.

(3) VR technology ☐.

① can only benefit children in the future

② is expected to become more realistic

③ should be used for specific fields

④ will bring significant benefits to us

Vocabulary & Grammar　重要表現や文法事項について理解しよう【知識】　　(英検®) (GTEC®)

Make the correct choice to complete each sentence.　(各3点)

(1) In addition (　　　) the food, we enjoyed the live music in the restaurant.

   ① for　　　　　② of　　　　　③ on　　　　　④ to

(2) Ted and Lucy kept (　　　) until it got dark.

   ① at walking　　② on walking　　③ to walk　　④ walk

(3) There are some experienced (　　　) and the latest facilities in the new hospital.

   ① supplies　　② surfaces　　③ surgeons　　④ surveys

(4) This problem is highly (　　　), so we need more time to solve it.

   ① comfort　　② complex　　③ concerned　　④ consistent

(5) Cherry blossoms (　　　) by many Japanese people for a long time.

   ① be loved　　② have been loved　　③ have loved　　④ loved

Listening　英文を聞いて理解しよう【知識・技能】【思考力・判断力・表現力】　　(共通テスト) 💿13

Listen to the English and make the best choice to match the content.　(4点)

   ① Esports may become one of the Olympic sports in the near future.

   ② Esports was announced to become an official Olympic sport.

   ③ The speaker is a popular esports player among young people.

Interaction　英文を聞いて会話を続けよう【知識・技能】【思考力・判断力・表現力】　　スピーキング・トレーナー

Listen to the English and respond to the last remark.　(7点)

〔メ モ　　　　　　　　　　　　　　　　　　　　　　　　　　　　　　　　　　〕

🔑 **Hints**
sightseeing (観光)，leisure activities (レジャー活動)，trip around the world (世界一周旅行)

Production (Speaking)　自分の考えを話して伝えよう【思考力・判断力・表現力】　　スピーキング・トレーナー

Answer the following question.　(9点)

Explain one negative aspect of a virtual trip.

〔メ モ　　　　　　　　　　　　　　　　　　　　　　　　　　　　　　　　　　〕

🔑 **Hints**
smell (臭い)，taste (味)，souvenir (土産)，Internet environment (インターネット環境)

With a **boxfish** on his head, / Sakana-kun often appears / on TV. // He is popular / for his cheerful **personality**. // Moreover, / he is respected / for his **knowledge** / of fish. //

    As a child, / Sakana-kun liked fish. // He also liked drawing. // He was
5 **obsessed** with drawing fish / and didn't study / at all. // His elementary school teacher asked his mother / to make him study. // But she answered, / "He really likes fish, / and I'm happy / with just the way he is." //

    His childhood dream / was to become an **ichthyology** professor. // Though he failed to enter university, / he worked hard / and **proved** himself / in the
10 ichthyology field. // Later, / he was invited / to join a university / as a visiting **associate** professor. // His consistent love for fish / enabled him to realize his dream. //

(124 words)

音読しよう　　　　　　　　　　　　　　　　　　　　　スピーキング・トレーナー

Practice 1 スラッシュ位置で文を区切って読んでみよう □
Practice 2 イントネーションに注意して読んでみよう □
TRY! 1分20秒以内に本文全体を音読しよう □

Reading　本文の内容を読んで理解しよう【知識・技能】【思考力・判断力・表現力】　　　共通テスト

Make the correct choice to complete each sentence or answer each question.　(各5点[(2)は完答])

(1) What special item does Sakana-kun have?　□
   ① He has a box made of fish bones.
   ② He has a boxfish on his right shoulder.
   ③ He wears a hat whose shape is like a fish.
   ④ He wears the same yellow jacket as the boxfish.

(2) Put the following events (①～④) into the order in which they happened.
   □ → □ → □ → □
   ① Sakana-kun became a visiting associate professor.
   ② Sakana-kun didn't study at all.
   ③ Sakana-kun studied hard and was recognized as a fish specialist.
   ④ Sakana-kun could not enter university.

(3) □ made his dream come true.
   ① Appearing on TV while wearing his fish hat　② Continuing to visit the professor
   ③ Great respect for his mother and fish　　　　④ His strong love for fish

Vocabulary & Grammar   重要表現や文法事項について理解しよう【知識】   英検® GTEC®

Make the correct choice to complete each sentence. （各3点）

(1) He is (   ) with tomorrow's exam.

　① observed　　　② obsessed　　　③ offered　　　④ organized

(2) You will have an opportunity to (   ) yourself if you keep working hard.

　① pour　　　② prepare　　　③ protect　　　④ prove

(3) Tom and Ted are twins but they have completely different (   ).

　① people　　　② person　　　③ personal　　　④ personalities

(4) Applicants for this job should have (   ) of biology and psychology.

　① alternative　　　② atmosphere　　　③ knowledge　　　④ neighborhood

(5) My mother said, "This song (   ) me of my childhood."

　① makes　　　② remains　　　③ remembers　　　④ reminds

Listening   英文を聞いて理解しよう【知識・技能】【思考力・判断力・表現力】   共通テスト 🔘14

Listen to the English and make the best choice to match the content. （4点）

　① Mike can explain economics in a way that people can easily understand.

　② Mike has a lot of knowledge about science technology.

　③ Mike is a well-known professor for his easy-to-understand explanations.

Interaction   英文を聞いて会話を続けよう【知識・技能】【思考力・判断力・表現力】   スピーキング・トレーナー

Listen to the English and respond to the last remark. （7点）

〔メモ　　　　　　　　　　　　　　　　　　　　　　　　　　　　　　　　　　〕

🎵 **Hints**
chat with friends（友達とおしゃべりする）, read comic books（マンガを読む）

Production（Speaking）   自分の考えを話して伝えよう【思考力・判断力・表現力】   スピーキング・トレーナー

Answer the following question. （9点）

Explain your friend's personality.

〔メモ　　　　　　　　　　　　　　　　　　　　　　　　　　　　　　　　　　〕

🎵 **Hints**
outgoing（社交的な）, talkative（おしゃべりな）, friendly（親しみやすい）, funny（面白い）

These are stairs / **decorated** like a piano. // We can actually make a piano-like sound / by stepping on the stairs. // This **motivates** us / to use the stairs / rather than the **escalator**. // Using the stairs / is not only fun / but also good / for our health. //

5　This **transparent trash bin** / allows us to see the garbage / inside it. // We are more likely to separate garbage **properly**; / otherwise we may look bad / to others / around us. // In addition, / we are more likely to follow the garbage **separation** rules / after seeing the garbage / already separated **correctly**. //

Just small **artifices** / like these / **evoke behavioral** changes / to solve personal or social problems. // They don't require **high-tech** devices / or lots of **expense**, / and they can change people's behaviors / for the better. //

(123 words)

音読しよう　　　　　　　　　　　　　　　　　　　スピーキング・トレーナー

Practice 1 スラッシュ位置で文を区切って読んでみよう ☐
Practice 2 イントネーションに注意して読んでみよう ☐
TRY! 1分20秒以内に本文全体を音読しよう ☐

Reading 本文の内容を読んで理解しよう【知識・技能】【思考力・判断力・表現力】　　共通テスト GTEC®

Make the correct choice to complete each sentence. （各5点）

(1) People ☐ the unique stairs rather than the escalator.
　　① avoid using　　② give up using　　③ refuse to use　　④ tend to use

(2) One **fact** from the article is that ☐.
　　① people don't separate garbage properly unless others are watching
　　② people who see correctly separated trash are more likely to follow the garbage separation rules
　　③ there are transparent trash bins
　　④ using the stairs with a piano-like sound is fun

(3) People can change their behaviors with ☐.
　　① some artifices that need lots of expense
　　② some tricks using high-tech devices
　　③ someone's small artworks
　　④ someone's small ideas

🎴 Vocabulary & Grammar　重要表現や文法事項について理解しよう【知識】　英検® GTEC®

Make the correct choice to complete each sentence.　（各3点）

(1) Please do not place items on the floor, otherwise I will (　　　) them.

①　step on　　　②　stop by　　　③　stretch to　　　④　supply for

(2) At the end of November, my family (　　　) our living room for Christmas.

①　decorates　　　②　dedicates　　　③　depends　　　④　divides

(3) The new stadium was built at great (　　　).

①　credit　　　②　exception　　　③　expense　　　④　money

(4) Negative words (　　　) negative emotions, so you shouldn't use them.

①　enable　　　②　evoke　　　③　memorize　　　④　motivate

(5) His expression (　　　) that he was not satisfied with the result.

①　showed　　　②　showing　　　③　shown　　　④　was shown

🎧 Listening　英文を聞いて理解しよう【知識・技能】【思考力・判断力・表現力】　共通テスト 💿15

Listen to the English and make the best choice to match the content.　（4点）

① The speaker believes that Japanese people should make more efforts to separate their garbage.

② The speaker says that Japan has the lowest recycling rate in the world.

③ The speaker thinks that Japan needs more landfills.

💬 Interaction　英文を聞いて会話を続けよう【知識・技能】【思考力・判断力・表現力】　スピーキング・トレーナー

Listen to the English and respond to the last remark.　（7点）

〔メモ　　〕

🔊 **Hints**

駅構内を何で移動することが多いか，理由とともに話してみましょう。

✏ Production（Writing）　自分の考えを書いて伝えよう【思考力・判断力・表現力】

Write your answer to the following question.　（9点）

What motivates you to study more?

──

──

🔊 **Hints**

favorite snacks（好きなおやつ），compete with friends for grades（友達と成績を競い合う）

Anju Niwata / and Professor Hidenori Watanave / have been involved / in the "**Rebooting** Memories" project. // This project aims to **inherit** memories of war / by **colorizing prewar** and **wartime** black-and-white photos. // These photos are colorized / **based** on AI technology / and conversations / with war survivors. //

5　In 2017, / as a high school student, / Anju met a man / who had experienced war / and listened to his story. // Soon after, / she learned / about **colorization** technology / in Watanave's workshop, / and then colorized his photos. // Seeing the colorized photos, / Anju and the man / felt a sense of **closeness** / to the past events / in the photos. //

10　These encounters led to their project. // They colorized photos / of people's daily lives / during wartime: / a family / under cherry blossoms / and a **couple** / **gazing** at a burnt-out city. // The people / in these photos / look alive, / as if they were actually in front of us. //

(141 words)

🔊 **音読しよう**　　　　　　　　　　　　　　　　　　　　　スピーキング・トレーナー

Practice 1 スラッシュ位置で文を区切って読んでみよう ☐
Practice 2 イントネーションに注意して読んでみよう ☐
TRY! 1分30秒以内に本文全体を音読しよう ☐

📖 **Reading** 本文の内容を読んで理解しよう【知識・技能】【思考力・判断力・表現力】　　共通テスト GTEC®

Make the correct choice to complete each sentence or answer each question. （各5点）

(1) What does "be involved in" mean in line 1? ☐
　① hold　　　　　② launch　　　　　③ organize　　　　　④ participate

(2) Which of the following is true? ☐
　① Anju has decided the color of the pictures by herself.
　② Some war survivors talked with AI to inherit memories of war.
　③ The original pictures used for the project are black-and-white.
　④ The pictures Watanave took during the war were used.

(3) One **opinion** from the article is that ☐.
　① Anju Niwata and Professor Hidenori Watanave have joined the "Rebooting Memories" project
　② several encounters led to this project
　③ the black-and-white photos are colorized using AI technology
　④ the people in the colorized pictures look alive

Vocabulary & Grammar 重要表現や文法事項について理解しよう【知識】 　英検® 　GTEC®

Make the correct choice to complete each sentence. （各3点）

(1) We have made our final decision based (　　　) various ideas.
　① at　　　　　　② in　　　　　　③ on　　　　　　④ with

(2) They say that Bob will (　　　) his father's business in the near future.
　① import　　　　② impress　　　　③ inherit　　　　④ insist

(3) Experiencing the same situations creates a sense of (　　　).
　① close　　　　② closely　　　　③ closeness　　　　④ closing

(4) The film director worked on (　　　) some black-and-white movies.
　① apologizing　　② colorizing　　③ nationalizing　　④ realizing

(5) I am very busy with our new project now. I wish I (　　　) to Hawaii to relax.
　① can go　　　　② could be gone　　③ could go　　　　④ go

Listening 英文を聞いて理解しよう【知識・技能】【思考力・判断力・表現力】 　共通テスト 　⊚16

Listen to the English and make the best choice to match the content. （4点）

① The speaker listened to speeches about war and peace at Hiroshima Peace Memorial Park.

② The speaker talked with war survivors last summer.

③ The speaker visited her grandparents in Hiroshima last summer.

Interaction 英文を聞いて会話を続けよう【知識・技能】【思考力・判断力・表現力】 　スピーキング・トレーナー

Listen to the English and respond to the last remark. （7点）

〔メモ 　　　　　　　　　　　　　　　　　　　　　　　　　　　　　　　　　　　　　　〕

🎧 **Hints**
お気に入りの写真について，現在進行形の文で描写してみよう。

Production (Writing) 自分の考えを書いて伝えよう【思考力・判断力・表現力】

Write your answer to the following question. （9点）

Describe a good memory from your childhood.

_____

_____

🎧 **Hints**
子供の頃好きだったおもちゃや遊び，一緒に遊んだ友達などを思い出し，そのときの気持ちも一緒に述べてみよう。

The WHO **officially** declared the world / free of **smallpox** / in 1980. // This was the result / of a WHO global **vaccination** campaign. // Today, / smallpox is the only infectious disease / that humans have **successfully eradicated**. // No effective **treatment** / for smallpox / exists, / and this **devastating** disease / killed

5　millions of people / in the past. //

There was a Japanese physician / who contributed to the global **eradication** / of smallpox. // He is Dr. Isao Arita. // He headed the WHO Smallpox Eradication **Unit** / from 1977 / to 1985. // He was awarded the Japan Prize / in 1988 / for this great contribution. // The **victory** / over smallpox / is considered / the most

10　**remarkable** achievement / in the history of international public health. //

(108 words)

🔊)) **音読しよう** 📖　　　　　　　　　　　　　　　スピーキング・トレーナー

Practice 1 スラッシュ位置で文を区切って読んでみよう ☐
Practice 2 イントネーションに注意して読んでみよう ☐
TRY! 1分10秒以内に本文全体を音読しよう ☐

📖 Reading 本文の内容を読んで理解しよう【知識・技能】【思考力・判断力・表現力】　　共通テスト GTEC®

Make the correct choice to complete each sentence or answer each question. （各5点）

(1) What does "declare" mean in line 1? ☐
　　① announce　　　② appreciate　　　③ influence　　　④ inspire

(2) Which of the following is **not** true? ☐
　　① In 1980, the WHO announced that smallpox had disappeared completely.
　　② Millions of people died because of smallpox.
　　③ The WHO started a global vaccination campaign against smallpox in 1980.
　　④ There was no effective treatment for smallpox in the past.

(3) Dr. Isao Arita ☐.
　　① received an award from the WHO because he made efforts to eradicate smallpox
　　② was a doctor who attempted to get rid of smallpox completely
　　③ was a Japanese physician who contributed to the development of the WHO
　　④ was the most remarkable physician in the history of international public health

🔖 Vocabulary & Grammar　重要表現や文法事項について理解しよう【知識】　英検® GTEC®

Make the correct choice to complete each sentence.　（各3点）

(1)　At this time of the year, I wish the world were free (　　　) pollen.
　　① in　　　　　　② of　　　　　　③ on　　　　　　④ to

(2)　My doctor told me, "You need some kind of (　　　) for this disease."
　　① effect　　　　② infection　　　③ recovery　　　④ treatment

(3)　Doctors are conducting various experiments to (　　　) the serious disease.
　　① employ　　　② encounter　　　③ eradicate　　　④ erupt

(4)　Amy was praised for her (　　　) test results this quarter.
　　① common　　　② miserable　　　③ related　　　④ remarkable

(5)　The city in (　　　) I lived ten years ago is in the western part of America.
　　① that　　　　　② what　　　　　③ which　　　　　④ who

🎧 Listening　英文を聞いて理解しよう【知識・技能】【思考力・判断力・表現力】　共通テスト 💿17

Listen to the English and make the best choice to match the content.　（4点）
　　① The speaker discusses his disease treatment with his physician.
　　② The speaker wants to help many patients as a nurse.
　　③ The speaker's dream is to become a doctor and research cures for diseases.

💬 Interaction　英文を聞いて会話を続けよう【知識・技能】【思考力・判断力・表現力】　スピーキング・トレーナー

Listen to the English and respond to the last remark.　（7点）
　　〔メ モ　　〕
　🔔 **Hints**
　　store food and water（食料や水を備蓄する），refrain from going out（外出を控える）

🗨 Production (Speaking)　自分の考えを話して伝えよう【思考力・判断力・表現力】　スピーキング・トレーナー

Answer the following question.　（9点）

Who do you think has achieved global success?　Why?
　　〔メ モ　　〕
　🔔 **Hints**
　　世界的に成功を収めていると思う人物とその理由を考えて話しましょう。

Just walk down a busy street / and look around / to see what's happening. // You will find / that many people are **glued** / to their smartphones. // These people may need a digital **detox**. //

A digital detox means / to **refrain** / from using electronic devices / connected
5 to the Internet, / such as smartphones and computers. // "Detoxing" from digital devices / is often seen / as a way / to focus on real-life social **interactions** / without **distractions**. //

You might feel anxious, / bored, / and even **annoyed** / without your smartphone / and other tech tools. // However, / a digital detox can be a **rewarding** experience /
10 that will help / to rest your exhausted brain, / relieve social media **fatigue**, / and improve the quality of sleep. // Why don't you put down your digital devices sometimes / and be **mindful** / of your other activities and experiences? // (128 words)

))) 音読しよう

スピーキング・トレーナー

Practice 1 スラッシュ位置で文を区切って読んでみよう ☐
Practice 2 イントネーションに注意して読んでみよう ☐
TRY! 1分25秒以内に本文全体を音読しよう ☐

📖 **Reading** 本文の内容を読んで理解しよう【知識・技能】【思考力・判断力・表現力】   共通テスト

Make the correct choice to complete each sentence or answer each question. (各5点)

(1) A digital detox ☐.
① may be needed by many people who walk down a busy street
② may be required by people who use their smartphones all the time
③ refers to people who are glued to their smartphones
④ refers to the use of electronic devices connected to the Internet

(2) Which of the following is true? ☐
① Digital detox may give you the latest information you want.
② Our brains will be activated by digital detox.
③ People can sleep better thanks to a digital detox.
④ You may feel social media fatigue with a digital detox.

(3) One **opinion** from the article is that ☐.
① a digital detox refers to not using electronic devices connected to the Internet
② using digital devices is a way to focus on real-life social interactions
③ you may feel unhappy when using your smartphone and other electronic devices
④ you should stop using your smartphone occasionally and enjoy your real life

🎴 Vocabulary & Grammar　重要表現や文法事項について理解しよう【知識】　英検® GTEC®

Make the correct choice to complete each sentence.　（各3点）

(1)　The notice in the museum says, "Please refrain (　　　　) taking photos here."

　① for　　　　② from　　　　③ on　　　　④ to

(2)　His rude attitude really (　　　　) me.

　① annoy　　　② annoyed　　　③ annoying　　　④ is annoyed

(3)　This big project is challenging but (　　　　) for me. I'll try it!

　① consistent　　② hard　　　③ rewarding　　　④ unnatural

(4)　According to the doctor, it is necessary to recover from both physical and mental (　　　　).

　① facility　　　② fatigue　　　③ figure　　　④ fortune

(5)　Bob has a toothache. He (　　　　) go to the dentist.

　① can　　　　② may　　　　③ might　　　　④ should

🎧 Listening　英文を聞いて理解しよう【知識・技能】【思考力・判断力・表現力】　共通テスト　💿18

Listen to the English and make the best choice to match the content.　（4点）

　① The speaker found it difficult to use the Internet.

　② The speaker is addicted to the latest online game.

　③ The speaker is talking about one social problem.

💬 Interaction　英文を聞いて会話を続けよう【知識・技能】【思考力・判断力・表現力】　スピーキング・トレーナー

Listen to the English and respond to the last remark.　（7点）

　〔メモ　　　　　　　　　　　　　　　　　　　　　　　　　　　　　　　　　〕

　🎧 **Hints**
　home telephone (家の電話)，picture post card (絵葉書)，send a letter (手紙を送る)，carrier pigeon (伝書バト)

😀 Production (Speaking)　自分の考えを話して伝えよう【思考力・判断力・表現力】　スピーキング・トレーナー

Answer the following question.　（9点）

What do you like to do on the Internet? How often do you usually do it in a day?

　〔メモ　　　　　　　　　　　　　　　　　　　　　　　　　　　　　　　　　〕

　🎧 **Hints**
　play online games (オンラインゲームをする)，check the website (ウェブサイトをチェックする)

A surprising amount of water / is used / in our daily lives. // The **term** "water **footprint**" / can be a good **indicator** / of this. // It refers to the amount of water / that is used and polluted / in order to produce the goods or services / we use. // A water footprint can be **calculated** / for any product. //

5　For **instance,** / a cup of coffee / needs 132 **liters** of water, / and one **margherita** pizza / requires 1,259 liters. // The water footprint / of one kilogram / of beef / is equal / to as much as 15,415 liters. // A pair of **jeans** / requires about 8,000 liters, / and one car requires 52,000–83,000 liters! //

It is important / to realize / that even though water is a limited resource, / we

10　depend on it so much / in every **aspect** of our lives. // The water footprint helps **visualize** this fact. //

(134 words)

🔊)) 音読しよう 📖 ━━━━━━━━━━━━━━━━━━ スピーキング・トレーナー

Practice 1 スラッシュ位置で文を区切って読んでみよう ☐
Practice 2 イントネーションに注意して読んでみよう ☐
TRY! 1分25秒以内に本文全体を音読しよう ☐

📖 **Reading** 本文の内容を読んで理解しよう【知識・技能】【思考力・判断力・表現力】 　(共通テスト)

Make the correct choice to complete each sentence or answer each question. (各5点[(2)は完答])

(1) The "water footprint" ☐.
　① can be a good indicator of a product's consumption
　② indicates the amount of water used to produce each product
　③ is calculated only for food products
　④ shows the water flow we can see

(2) Put the following options from the highest to the lowest water footprints.
　☐ → ☐ → ☐ → ☐
　① a pair of jeans　　　② one car　　　③ one kilogram of beef　　　④ one pizza

(3) One **opinion** from the article is that ☐.
　① it requires a significant amount of water to produce something
　② people should remember that water is limited
　③ water footprints reveal hidden water-related issues
　④ we use a lot of water in our daily lives

🔖 Vocabulary & Grammar　重要表現や文法事項について理解しよう【知識】　英検® GTEC®

Make the correct choice to complete each sentence. （各3点）

(1) (　　　　) Cathy studied very hard, she didn't pass the examination.

① Even if 　　　② Even though 　　　③ In case 　　　④ Unless

(2) You must read the textbook about legal (　　　　) to become a lawyer.

① tales 　　　② tellers 　　　③ terms 　　　④ trails

(3) Dean needed to (　　　　) the expenses and submit the document after his business trip, but he didn't.

① calculate 　　　② capture 　　　③ chat 　　　④ conflict

(4) Setting your ID and password is a key (　　　　) of using the Internet.

① account 　　　② adapt 　　　③ angle 　　　④ aspect

(5) Can you help me (　　　　) for my move this Saturday?

① be prepared 　　　② prepare 　　　③ prepared 　　　④ preparing

🎧 Listening　英文を聞いて理解しよう【知識・技能】【思考力・判断力・表現力】　共通テスト 💿19

Listen to the English and make the best choice to match the content. （4点）

① Children in developing countries cannot go to school because of poverty.

② Getting clean water is a big problem in some developing countries.

③ In some developing countries, it takes more than an hour to get water.

💬 Interaction　英文を聞いて会話を続けよう【知識・技能】【思考力・判断力・表現力】　スピーキング・トレーナー

Listen to the English and respond to the last remark. （7点）

〔メモ 　　　　　　　　　　　　　　　　　　　　　　　　　　　　　　　　　　　　　　〕

🎧 **Hints**
population (人口)，demand (需要)，climate change (気候変動)，deforestation (森林伐採)，agriculture (農業)

✍️ Production（Writing）　自分の考えを書いて伝えよう【思考力・判断力・表現力】

Write your answer to the following question. （9点）

Explain one thing you can do to save water.

_____

_____

🎧 **Hints**
自分の生活を思い返し，節水のためにできることを考えてみましょう。

The Earth is surrounded / by **countless** pieces of waste / called "space debris." // They are parts / of **abandoned** rocket bodies / and **satellites**. // It is **estimated** / that there are more than 100 million pieces / of space debris / **orbiting** around the Earth. //

5 Space debris travels / at about eight kilometers / per second. // If it hits and damages satellites / used for climate research, / **telecommunications** / and **navigation**, / it will lead to serious **consequences**. //

Researchers have been studying ways / to remove space debris. // For example, / they have developed a **remotely** controlled vehicle / and a space net

10 satellite / designed to capture debris. // However, / debris **removal** technology / has not yet been put into practical use. // Further international **cooperation** / will be necessary / for sustainable space development. //   (116 words)

 音読しよう   スピーキング・トレーナー

Practice 1 スラッシュ位置で文を区切って読んでみよう ☐
Practice 2 イントネーションに注意して読んでみよう ☐
TRY! 1分15秒以内に本文全体を音読しよう ☐

Reading 本文の内容を読んで理解しよう【知識・技能】【思考力・判断力・表現力】   (共通テスト)

Make the correct choice to complete each sentence or answer each question. (各5点)

(1) Which of the following is **not** true? ☐
  ① Researchers have attempted to create as much space debris as possible.
  ② Space debris consists of parts of rockets and satellites that don't work.
  ③ Space debris moves at about eight kilometers per second.
  ④ There are millions of pieces of space debris around the Earth.

(2) When space debris hits a satellite, there is a possibility that ☐ .
  ① climate change is more likely to occur
  ② only cellphone companies are affected
  ③ we can talk on the phone for free
  ④ we may get lost while driving a car

(3) One **opinion** from the article is that ☐ .
  ① international cooperation will be needed for the growth of the space industry
  ② researchers have developed a remotely controlled vehicle and a space net satellite
  ③ the countless pieces of waste around the Earth are called "space debris"
  ④ there is countless space debris around the Earth

Goals

🔊 イントネーションを理解して音読することができる。 📖 宇宙ごみの問題に関する英文を読んで概要や要点をとらえることができる。
📝 文脈を理解して適切な語句を用いて英文を完成することができる。 🎧 平易な英語で話される短い英文を聞いて必要な情報を聞き取ることができる。
💬 宇宙でしたいことについて簡単な語句を用いて情報や考えを伝えることができる。 ✍ 宇宙開発の問題点について簡単な語句を用いて考えを表現することができる。

✏ Vocabulary & Grammar 重要表現や文法事項について理解しよう【知識】 英検® GTEC®

Make the correct choice to complete each sentence. （各3点）

(1) Do you know when this study will be put into (　　　) use?

① positive　　② potential　　③ practical　　④ prepared

(2) According to the guide, the tree is (　　　) to be over one thousand years old.

① estimated　　② exposed　　③ expressed　　④ extended

(3) Politicians in this country should deeply regret the devastating (　　　) of war.

① comprehensions　② confidences　③ consequences　④ constructions

(4) Some members of the IT group can access all employees' computers (　　　) to perform updates.

① approximately　② extremely　③ remotely　④ dramatically

(5) My grandfather (　　　) Mt. Fuji since sunrise.

① climbed　　② has been climbed　③ has been climbing　④ has climbed

🎧 Listening 英文を聞いて理解しよう【知識・技能】【思考力・判断力・表現力】 共通テスト 💿20

Listen to the English and make the best choice to match the content. （4点）

① The speaker is explaining how a pair of jeans is made and thrown away.

② The speaker is talking about one company's efforts in recycling.

③ The speaker is trying to recycle clothes at the shop.

💬 Interaction 英文を聞いて会話を続けよう【知識・技能】【思考力・判断力・表現力】 スピーキング・トレーナー

Listen to the English and respond to the last remark. （7点）

〔メ モ 　　　　　　　　　　　　　　　　　　　　　　　　　　　　　　　　　　 〕

👆 **Hints**
Mars (火星), emigrate (移住する), alien (宇宙人), weightlessness／zero gravity (無重力)

✍ Production (Writing) 自分の考えを書いて伝えよう【思考力・判断力・表現力】

Write your answer to the following question. （9点）

What do you think are the problems with space development?

_____

_____

👆 **Hints**
unknown (未知の), enormous expense (莫大な費用), astronaut (宇宙飛行士)

In the **animated** movie, / *Tenkinoko* / (*Weathering with You*), / it continues to rain / for over two years, / and as a result / the city of Tokyo is changed a lot. // Could this actually happen / in real life? //

It's unlikely / that it would rain **continuously** / for so long. // In fact, / the
5 **annual precipitation** of Tokyo / has **barely** changed at all / over the last thirty years. // On the other hand, / however, / it is a fact / that **abnormal** weather / such as heavy **downpours** / is becoming more **frequent** / in Japan. // There have been increasing cases / of heavy **rainfall** / causing serious damage. //

One of the factors / behind such abnormal weather / is global warming. //
10 If we can't stop global warming, / the **frequency** of heavy downpours / may increase more and more. // Now / we must take more steps / to fight against global warming / and to protect the Earth. //

(138 words)

🔊)) **音読しよう** 📖 ～～～～～～～～～ **スピーキング・トレーナー**

Practice 1 スラッシュ位置で文を区切って読んでみよう ☐
Practice 2 イントネーションに注意して読んでみよう ☐
TRY! 1分30秒以内に本文全体を音読しよう ☐

📖 **Reading** 本文の内容を読んで理解しよう【知識・技能】【思考力・判断力・表現力】 共通テスト GTEC®

Make the correct choice to complete each sentence or answer each question. （各5点）

(1) What does "frequent" mean in line 7? ☐
　① appropriate　　② often　　③ random　　④ unexpected

(2) Which of the following is **not** true? ☐
　① Heavy rains have resulted in significant damage.
　② *Tenkinoko* (*Weathering with You*) describes an unusual climate in Tokyo.
　③ The annual rainfall in Tokyo has remained nearly the same over the last 30 years.
　④ The number of heavy downpours in Japan is decreasing.

(3) One **fact** from the article is that ☐.
　① if we cannot stop global warming, heavy rain may occur more frequently
　② it's unlikely that it would rain continuously for two years
　③ one of the reasons for abnormal weather is global warming
　④ we must take steps to fight against global warming

📝 Vocabulary & Grammar　重要表現や文法事項について理解しよう【知識】　　英検® GTEC®

Make the correct choice to complete each sentence.　(各3点)

(1) We must (　　　) steps to prevent crimes.

① bury　　　　　② carry　　　　　③ gain　　　　　④ take

(2) Our sports day is an (　　　) autumn event that everyone looks forward to.

① annual　　　　② enormous　　　　③ instant　　　　④ unnatural

(3) I am sorry, but I could (　　　) understand what you said.

① barely　　　　② constantly　　　　③ regularly　　　　④ sharply

(4) Lately, he has been suffering from (　　　) headaches.

① always　　　　② frequent　　　　③ often　　　　④ usually

(5) Tom had an opinion (　　　) the new construction plan would not be adopted.

① so that　　　　② that　　　　③ what　　　　④ which

🎧 Listening　英文を聞いて理解しよう【知識・技能】【思考力・判断力・表現力】　　共通テスト 🔘21

Listen to the English and make the best choice to match the content.　(4点)

① The speaker doesn't like wearing a raincoat on rainy days.

② The speaker is talking about her habit.

③ The speaker will take her dog for a walk later.

💬 Interaction　英文を聞いて会話を続けよう【知識・技能】【思考力・判断力・表現力】　　スピーキング・トレーナー

Listen to the English and respond to the last remark.　(7点)

〔メモ　　　　　　　　　　　　　　　　　　　　　　　　　　　　　　　　　　　　　　　〕

🎤 **Hints**

one's birthday party (…の誕生日会)，(Saint) Valentine's Day (バレンタインデー)，the *Bon* festival (盆祭り)

🗣 Production (Speaking)　自分の考えを話して伝えよう【思考力・判断力・表現力】　　スピーキング・トレーナー

Answer the following question.　(9点)

Recommend your favorite animated movie or cartoon.

〔メモ　　　　　　　　　　　　　　　　　　　　　　　　　　　　　　　　　　　　　　　〕

🎤 **Hints**

好きなアニメ作品について，理由とともに話してみよう。

No Rain, No Rainbow

❶ The accident happened / in 2006, / when I was 18. // On my way home, / my motorcycle **collided** / with a car. // After a 12-hour-long **surgery**, / I barely survived. // However, / I was told / that I would spend the rest of my life / **confined** to bed. //

5 **❷** After six months / of **physical rehabilitation**, / I had learned to do many things / by myself / in a wheelchair. // Then, / I moved to another rehabilitation center, / where I met my **mentor** / in life. // He was **undergoing** rehabilitation / in the center, / too. // He always said to me, / "Opportunity is under your feet. // All you need to do / is recognize it." // He gave me several missions / 10 to **accomplish**, / like going back home alone / on the train. // **Completing** the missions / he had given me, / I gradually gained confidence / in myself. // Finally, / leaving the rehabilitation center / in 2009, / I decided to live alone. //

(140 words)

🔊 **音読しよう** 📖 〜〜〜〜〜〜〜〜〜〜〜〜〜 スピーキング・トレーナー

Practice 1 スラッシュ位置で文を区切って読んでみよう ☐
Practice 2 英語の音の変化に注意して読んでみよう ☐
TRY! 1分20秒以内に本文全体を音読しよう ☐

📖 **Reading** 本文の内容を読んで理解しよう【知識・技能】【思考力・判断力・表現力】 （共通テスト）

Make the correct choice to complete each sentence. （各5点）

(1) In 2006, Tatsuya Miyo ☐.

① had a 12-hour-long brain surgery

② hit a motorcycle on his way to school

③ was confined to his car because of a traffic accident

④ was informed that he would stay in bed for the rest of his life

(2) Tatsuya's mentor wanted him to ☐.

① accomplish something on his own

② go home with him on the train

③ learn to do many things in the rehabilitation center

④ ride a motorcycle again

(3) After Tatsuya met his mentor, ☐.

① he became more confident because of the challenges his mentor gave him

② he left the rehabilitation center and decided to travel alone

③ he moved to another rehabilitation center with him

④ he spent most of the time confined to bed

🎴 Vocabulary & Grammar　重要表現や文法事項について理解しよう【知識】　英検® GTEC®

Make the correct choice to complete each sentence.　（各3点）

(1) Ken's bike nearly (　　　　) with the parked car because he was riding it while using his smartphone.

　① calculated　　　② collided　　　③ completed　　　④ confused

(2) The dentist often tells me that I should (　　　) a dental examination twice a year.

　① undergo　　　② understand　　　③ unite　　　④ unveil

(3) He overcame a lot of difficulties to (　　　) his task.

　① accept　　　② accomplish　　　③ announce　　　④ attend

(4) Preparations for the presentation have already been (　　　　).

　① competed　　　② completed　　　③ conserved　　　④ contributed

(5) The man said to me, "(　　　) you have to do is sign here."

　① All　　　② All of　　　③ That　　　④ Which

🎧 Listening　英文を聞いて理解しよう【知識・技能】【思考力・判断力・表現力】　共通テスト 💿22

Listen to the English and make the best choice to match the content.　（4点）

　① The number of car accidents on First Street has decreased.

　② The speaker had a car accident this morning.

　③ There was a traffic accident, but nobody got hurt.

💬 Interaction　英文を聞いて会話を続けよう【知識・技能】【思考力・判断力・表現力】　スピーキング・トレーナー

Listen to the English and respond to the last remark.　（7点）

〔メ モ　　　　　　　　　　　　　　　　　　　　　　　　　　　　　　　　　　〕

🎵 **Hints**
take someone to ... (…へ連れて行く), lead the way to ... (…へ案内する), elevator (エレベーター)

✍ Production (Writing)　自分の考えを書いて伝えよう【思考力・判断力・表現力】

Write your answer to the following question.　（9点）

Who do you want to be your mentor? Why?

🎵 **Hints**
have a great career (素晴らしいキャリアがある), be in the same position (同じ立場にいる), encourage (…を勇気づける)

No Rain, No Rainbow

❸ In 2011, / I traveled to Hawaii alone. // It seemed like an enormous challenge, / but my friends gave me a push. // I enjoyed Hawaii / to the fullest, / which led to my next challenge: / a **journey** / around the world. //

❹ I left Japan / in 2017 / and had **fortunate** encounters / during the journey. //

5 Once, / my wheelchair got broken / on a stone **pavement** / in Florence, / Italy. // Then, / an Italian family / passing nearby / offered me help / and **struggled** to fix it / for me. // How lucky I was! //

❺ I visited 23 countries / in nine months. // Through the journey, / I found / the world was still full of physical **barriers**. // At the same time, / I found / these

10 barriers could be overcome / with the **kindness** of others. // The motorcycle accident was a "rain" / in my life, / but thanks to that rain, / I encountered many "rainbows" / — wonderful people / in the world. //

(140 words)

🔊))) 音読しよう 📖   スピーキング・トレーナー

Practice 1 スラッシュ位置で文を区切って読んでみよう ☐
Practice 2 英語の音の変化に注意して読んでみよう ☐
TRY! 1分20秒以内に本文全体を音読しよう ☐

📖 **Reading** 本文の内容を読んで理解しよう【知識・技能】【思考力・判断力・表現力】   共通テスト

Make the correct choice to complete each sentence or answer each question. (各5点)

(1) Tatsuya ☐.

① broke his wheelchair on the pavement during a trip to Hawaii
② decided on Hawaii as the first country for his journey around the world
③ enjoyed his trip to Hawaii by himself, so he set a new goal
④ traveled to Hawaii with his friends and enjoyed it very much

(2) Which of the following is true? ☐

① An Italian family asked a bike store worker to repair Tatsuya's wheelchair.
② Tatsuya spent over a year traveling to 23 countries.
③ Tatsuya was helped by some local people in Italy.
④ Tatsuya's wheelchair got broken on a stone bridge.

(3) After traveling around the world, Tatsuya found that ☐.

① many physical barriers could be overcome with the help of kind people
② the motorcycle accident was a "rain" in his life and his experiences were "rainbows"
③ there were a lot of wonderful people in Italy
④ traveling to Hawaii alone seemed like a big challenge

英語の音の変化を理解して音読することができる。　三代さんが感じたことに関する英文を読んで概要や要点をとらえることができる。
文脈を理解して適切な語句を用いて英文を完成することができる。　平易な英語で話される短い英文を聞いて必要な情報を聞き取ることができる。
旅での特別な思い出について簡単な語句を用いて情報や考えを伝えることができる。　自分にとっての "rain", "rainbow" について簡単な語句を用いて考えを表現することができる。

Vocabulary & Grammar　重要表現や文法事項について理解しよう【知識】　英検® GTEC®

Make the correct choice to complete each sentence.　（各3点）

(1) He (　　　) to find his lost wedding ring before his wife returned.
① earned　　② scared　　③ served　　④ struggled

(2) I was (　　　) to have good friends during my high school years.
① fortunate　　② fortunately　　③ fortune　　④ unfortunately

(3) Be careful not to slip on the (　　　) when walking on a snowy day.
① burden　　② fate　　③ pavement　　④ process

(4) His last words were, "Enjoy your life to the (　　　)."
① fulfill　　② fulfilled　　③ fullest　　④ fullness

(5) Susan argued loudly with her classmate yesterday, (　　　) surprised us a lot because she is usually quiet.
① that　　② what　　③ which　　④ who

Listening　英文を聞いて理解しよう【知識・技能】【思考力・判断力・表現力】　共通テスト　23

Listen to the English and make the best choice to match the content.　（4点）

① In the new shopping mall, there are two restrooms on each floor.
② The new shopping mall seems to be convenient for wheelchair users.
③ The speaker is talking about a new shop in the shopping mall.

Interaction　英文を聞いて会話を続けよう【知識・技能】【思考力・判断力・表現力】　スピーキング・トレーナー

Listen to the English and respond to the last remark.　（7点）

〔メモ　　　　　　　　　　　　　　　　　　　　　　　　　　　〕

Hints
旅での特別な思い出について答えましょう。

Production（Speaking）　自分の考えを話して伝えよう【思考力・判断力・表現力】　スピーキング・トレーナー

Answer the following question.　（9点）

The motorcycle accident was like a "rain" and wonderful people in the world were "rainbows" for Tatsuya Miyo. Explain your "rain" and "rainbow" in your life.

〔メモ　　　　　　　　　　　　　　　　　　　　　　　　　　　〕

Hints
自分にとっての "rain", "rainbow" について話してみよう。

Interviewer : I've heard / you're starting a new life / in Okinawa. // Could you tell me why? //

Tatsuya : First of all, / I love Okinawa. // I'm **fascinated** / by the amazing nature / and the kindness / of the people there. // Also, / Okinawa gives high **priority** /

5　to **universal** tourism, / which is **accessible** to all people / **regardless** of age, / nationality / and **disability**. // There are things / I want to report on / as a wheelchair traveler. //

Interviewer : I see. // I'm looking forward to reading your report soon. //

Tatsuya : Thank you. //

10　*Interviewer :* You've challenged yourself / in many things / in your life / so far. // What would you like to say / to those who are hesitating / to take a step forward / like you? //

Tatsuya : Well, / I understand / you'll feel anxious / when you start something new. // Just take it easy. // People around you / are watching your efforts. //

15　They're ready / to help you. //

(133 words)

音読しよう 📖　　　　　　　　　　　　　　　スピーキング・トレーナー

Practice 1 スラッシュ位置で文を区切って読んでみよう ☐

Practice 2 英語の音の変化に注意して読んでみよう ☐

TRY! 1分15秒以内に本文全体を音読しよう ☐

📖 Reading 本文の内容を読んで理解しよう【知識・技能】【思考力・判断力・表現力】　共通テスト GTEC®

Make the correct choice to complete each sentence or answer each question. （各5点）

(1) Universal tourism ____.

① benefits people, particularly those in wheelchairs

② brings Japanese people into amazing locations in nature

③ enables all people to enjoy traveling

④ is a unique style of tourism in Okinawa

(2) What does "anxious" mean in line 13? ____

① comfortable　　　　② nervous　　　　③ rude　　　　④ thrilling

(3) One **opinion** from the interview is that ____.

① the people around you will help you when you are in trouble

② you might be anxious before you travel

③ you should watch the efforts of the people around you

④ we must be kind to help those people in need

Vocabulary & Grammar　重要表現や文法事項について理解しよう【知識】　(英検®)(GTEC®)

Make the correct choice to complete each sentence.　(各3点)

(1) The audience at the concert was (　　　) not only by the song but also by her voice.
① excellent　② fascinated　③ fluent　④ valued

(2) Railroad companies should give first (　　　) to the safety of their passengers.
① passage　② pause　③ priority　④ property

(3) Our new computer system has been installed since last Monday. There haven't been any problems (　　　).
① as far as　② by far　③ so far　④ so further

(4) This school offers some courses to provide job opportunities for people with (　　　).
① definitions　② demonstrations　③ destructions　④ disabilities

(5) I am really looking forward to (　　　) your wedding ceremony in two weeks.
① attend　② attending　③ be attended　④ have attending

Listening　英文を聞いて理解しよう【知識・技能】【思考力・判断力・表現力】　(共通テスト) 24

Listen to the English and make the best choice to match the content.　(4点)
① New things make the speaker nervous.
② The speaker always makes an effort to do something new.
③ The speaker's sister feels nervous when she starts something new.

Interaction　英文を聞いて会話を続けよう【知識・技能】【思考力・判断力・表現力】　スピーキング・トレーナー

Listen to the English and respond to the remarks.　(7点)

〔メモ　　　　　　　　　　　　　　　　　　　　　　　　　　　　　〕

🎵**Hints**
ramp (スロープ), braille block (点字ブロック), blind people (目の不自由な人), deaf people (耳の不自由な人)

Production (Writing)　自分の考えを書いて伝えよう【思考力・判断力・表現力】

Write your answer to the following question.　(9点)
Which place do you think gives high priority to universal tourism?

_____

_____

🎵**Hints**
ユニバーサルツーリズムに重点を置いていると思う場所と，その理由を書いてみましょう。

1 In a village / in Bangladesh, / a man puts a **spoonful** of white **powder** / into a **beaker** / of dirty water / taken from a local pond. // He **stirs** it / and the water becomes clear / in a few minutes. // He then **filters** the water / and drinks it. // People say, / "That powder is magic!" //

5 **2** The man's name / is Kanetoshi Oda. // In 1995, / he experienced the Great Hanshin-Awaji Earthquake. // At the time of that disaster, / **tap** water was cut off / and many people were in trouble. // He thought, / "How helpful it would be / if we could use **muddy** pond water / for drinking." //

3 The solution was unexpectedly close at hand. // He remembered / that the 10 **sticky** component / in *natto* / — **polyglutamic acid** / — can **purify** water. // He spent years / experimenting in his **lab** / and finally succeeded / in developing water purifying powder / from polyglutamic acid. //

(135 words)

🔊 **音読しよう**   スピーキング・トレーナー

Practice 1 スラッシュ位置で文を区切って読んでみよう ☐
Practice 2 英語の音の変化に注意して読んでみよう ☐
TRY! 1分20秒以内に本文全体を音読しよう ☐

📖 **Reading** 本文の内容を読んで理解しよう【知識・技能】【思考力・判断力・表現力】   共通テスト GTEC®

Make the correct choice to complete each sentence or answer each question. （各5点）

(1) What does "component" mean in line 10? ☐
  ① element   ② material   ③ mineral   ④ texture

(2) ☐ was one of the biggest problems when there was an earthquake in 1995.
  ① Cooking with muddy pond water
  ② Drinking dirty water from local ponds
  ③ Lack of fresh water
  ④ Purifying water with some magic powder

(3) Which of the following is **not** true? ☐
  ① Oda got some ideas from his experience with the Great Hanshin-Awaji Earthquake.
  ② Oda knew some difficulties caused by the disaster.
  ③ Oda used the white powder to purify the water in a village in Bangladesh.
  ④ Oda was in Bangladesh in 1995.

Vocabulary & Grammar　重要表現や文法事項について理解しよう【知識】　英検® GTEC®

Make the correct choice to complete each sentence. （各3点）

(1) After cracking the eggs, add the sugar and (　　　) well.

① bore　　　② power　　　③ sour　　　④ stir

(2) Do you usually drink (　　　) water or mineral water?

① tab　　　② tag　　　③ tap　　　④ tax

(3) Sam is very kind. I often see him helping people who are (　　　).

① at problems　　　② in problems　　　③ in trouble　　　④ to trouble

(4) The new appliance can (　　　) the air in the large room.

① allow　　　② enter　　　③ purify　　　④ set

(5) If Tom and Sally (　　　) here, I could tell them that interesting story right now.

① are　　　② was　　　③ were　　　④ will be

Listening　英文を聞いて理解しよう【知識・技能】【思考力・判断力・表現力】　共通テスト　◉25

Listen to the English and make the best choice to match the content. （4点）

① Some people could not evacuate because the shelters were full.

② The speaker is delivering the news about the earthquake.

③ The speaker reported that there was no damage from the earthquake.

Interaction　英文を聞いて会話を続けよう【知識・技能】【思考力・判断力・表現力】　スピーキング・トレーナー

Listen to the English and respond to the last remark. （7点）

〔メモ　　　　　　　　　　　　　　　　　　　　　　　　　　　　　　　　　　　　　　〕

🎧 **Hints**

water quality（水質），an adoption rate for ...（…の普及率），leak（漏れる），infrastructure（インフラ，社会基盤施設）

Production（Writing）　自分の考えを書いて伝えよう【思考力・判断力・表現力】

Write your answer to the following question. （9点）

What do you think we should prepare for when the water supply is cut off?

✍ **Hints**

water tank（給水タンク），bottled water（ペットボトルに入った飲料水），wet wipes（ウェットティッシュ）

4 Unfortunately, / Oda's water **purifier** didn't sell well / in Japan. // However, / in 2004, / when the Sumatra-Andaman Earthquake occurred, / it was **adopted** / to help victims / in Thailand. // This attracted global attention / and it was **subsequently** used / in other countries / such as Mexico, / Bangladesh / and

5 Somalia. //

5 Oda thought / just selling his product / was **insufficient**, / however. // So, / he taught the local people / how to **effectively** market it / in order to create sustainable businesses. // This has given them / both a steady supply of water / and new **employment**. // It has also improved their quality of life. //

10 **6** Oda's water purifier is now sold / in over 40 countries / and provides safe **drinkable** water / to about 2.8 million people. // He says, / "Now I know / what I was born for. // While I am alive, / I wish to create a world / where everyone can get safe water." //

(136 words)

🔊)) **音読しよう** 📖 〜〜〜〜〜〜〜〜〜〜〜〜〜〜 スピーキング・トレーナー

Practice 1 スラッシュ位置で文を区切って読んでみよう ☐
Practice 2 英語の音の変化に注意して読んでみよう ☐
TRY! 1分20秒以内に本文全体を音読しよう ☐

📖 Reading　本文の内容を読んで理解しよう【知識・技能】【思考力・判断力・表現力】　共通テスト GTEC®

Make the correct choice to complete each sentence or answer each question. （各5点[(3)は完答]）

(1) What does "attract" mean in line 3?　☐

　① draw　　　　② estimate　　　　③ focus　　　　④ recognize

(2) As a result of being taught how to sell the water purifier, local people ☐.

　① decided to improve their quality of life on their own
　② have received several benefits, and their quality of life has improved
　③ let Oda get a steady supply of water and new employment
　④ succeeded in developing their own water purifiers

(3) Put the following events (①〜④) into the order in which they happened.

　☐ → ☐ → ☐ → ☐

　① People around the world became very interested in the water purifier.
　② The Sumatra-Andaman Earthquake occurred, and the water purifier was used to help people in Thailand.
　③ The water purifier has provided clean water to more than 2 million people worldwide.
　④ The water purifier made by Oda didn't sell well in Japan.

📇 Vocabulary & Grammar　重要表現や文法事項について理解しよう【知識】　英検® GTEC®

Make the correct choice to complete each sentence.　（各 3 点）

(1) A famous singer (　　　　) a song and lyrics to a new singer.

① asked　　　　② provided　　　　③ rejected　　　　④ stretched

(2) Some new employees seem to have the ability to work (　　　　).

① absolutely　　　② differently　　　③ effectively　　　④ obviously

(3) Tim gave a speech about the (　　　　) food supply and the need for assistance in some developing countries.

① imitational　　　② impressive　　　③ included　　　④ insufficient

(4) New policies were introduced and the company's performance (　　　　) improved.

① politely　　　② remotely　　　③ subsequently　　　④ unfortunately

(5) (　　　　), the hurricane didn't approach this city and there was no damage.

① Clearly　　　② Fortunately　　　③ Naturally　　　④ Sadly

🎧 Listening　英文を聞いて理解しよう【知識・技能】【思考力・判断力・表現力】　共通テスト ◎ 26

Listen to the English and make the best choice to match the content.　（4 点）

① Malaysia has fewer water resources than Singapore.

② Singapore has found a solution to its water shortage.

③ The Singapore government has decided to stop importing water from Malaysia.

💬 Interaction　英文を聞いて会話を続けよう【知識・技能】【思考力・判断力・表現力】　スピーキング・トレーナー

Listen to the English and respond to the last remark.　（7 点）

〔メモ　　　　　　　　　　　　　　　　　　　　　　　　　　　　　　　　　　　　　　〕

🎙 **Hints**
水道設備が整っていない国での生活を想像し，どのような問題が生じるかを考えて話してみましょう。

🗨 Production（Speaking）　自分の考えを話して伝えよう【思考力・判断力・表現力】　スピーキング・トレーナー

Answer the following question.　（9 点）

What do you think is necessary to work abroad?

〔メモ　　　　　　　　　　　　　　　　　　　　　　　　　　　　　　　　　　　　　　〕

🎙 **Hints**
ability to ～（～する能力），flexible（柔軟な），cooperative（協力的な），sense of responsibility（責任感）

In developing countries, / there are still many people / who cannot get safe drinking water. // Building water wells / might be one way / to help these people. // However, / there are some points / that need to be considered. //

1. Just building water wells / is not enough. //

5　　Water wells sometimes stop being used / when the **equipment** gets broken. // In some cases, / equipment parts are stolen / to be sold / for profit. // It is important / to find ways / in which local people can use and manage the wells **sustainably**. // We need to have a long-term **perspective**. //

2. Situations **differ** / from place to place. //

10　　Some places **urgently** need wells / to **secure** water, / while others need developed water supply systems / rather than wells. // We have to **grasp** the actual situations / and provide **adequate** support / that meets the needs / of each case. //

(133 words)

音読しよう　　　　　　　　　　　　　　　　スピーキング・トレーナー

Practice 1 スラッシュ位置で文を区切って読んでみよう ☐
Practice 2 英語の音の変化に注意して読んでみよう ☐
TRY! 1分15秒以内に本文全体を音読しよう ☐

Reading

本文の内容を読んで理解しよう【知識・技能】【思考力・判断力・表現力】　　　共通テスト　GTEC®

Make the correct choice to complete each sentence or answer each question. （各5点）

(1) What does "profit" mean in line 6? ☐
　　① benefit　　　　② charity　　　　③ innovation　　　　④ property

(2) Which of the following is true? ☐
　　① Although situations differ from place to place, the same support will be needed.
　　② Building water wells is easier than developing water supply systems.
　　③ It is necessary to provide appropriate support by considering the local conditions.
　　④ Water wells are one of the tools for sustainable water supply.

(3) One **fact** from the article is that ☐.
　　① building water wells may be one method to help people
　　② it is important for local people to find ways to manage their wells sustainably
　　③ water wells are sometimes not used when the equipment becomes damaged
　　④ we must understand the actual situations of people who have trouble getting clean water

Goals

🔊 英語の音の変化を理解して音読することができる。　📖 井戸建設に関するウェブサイトを読んで概要や要点をとらえることができる。
📝 文脈を理解して適切な語句を用いて英文を完成することができる。　🎧 平易な英語で話される短い英文を聞いて必要な情報を聞き取ることができる。
🗣 水道設備の恩恵について簡単な語句を用いて情報や考えを伝えることができる。　✍ 海外ボランティアについて簡単な語句を用いて考えを表現することができる。

🔖 Vocabulary & Grammar　重要表現や文法事項について理解しよう【知識】　英検® GTEC®

Make the correct choice to complete each sentence.　(各3点)

(1) The young photographer has to climb the mountain with some heavy camera (　　　).
　　① equipment　　② evidence　　③ furniture　　④ service

(2) Mike gave us some valuable advice from the (　　　) of an engineer.
　　① percentage　　② perspective　　③ preparation　　④ preservation

(3) Visitors must (　　　) permission at the front desk in advance.
　　① admit　　② attend　　③ secure　　④ settle

(4) It is often difficult for us to (　　　) his unique ideas.
　　① gasp　　② grasp　　③ gratitude　　④ guard

(5) Some like English, and (　　　) like mathematics.
　　① another　　② other　　③ others　　④ the others

🎧 Listening　英文を聞いて理解しよう【知識・技能】【思考力・判断力・表現力】　共通テスト　27

Listen to the English and make the best choice to match the content.　(4点)

① Japan has a lot of wells to secure drinking water now.

② Some local governments have found it useful to use wells during natural disasters.

③ The number of Japanese people who do not know how to use wells is decreasing.

💬 Interaction　英文を聞いて会話を続けよう【知識・技能】【思考力・判断力・表現力】　スピーキング・トレーナー

Listen to the English and respond to the last remark.　(7点)

〔メモ　　　　　　　　　　　　　　　　　　　　　　　　　　　　　　　　　　　　　　　〕

🎤 **Hints**
be good for the health (健康によい)，improve (…を改善する)，draw water (水を汲む)

✍ Production (Writing)　自分の考えを書いて伝えよう【思考力・判断力・表現力】

Write your answer to the following question.　(9点)

Imagine that you work in a local area in Bangladesh as a volunteer. How would you grasp the local people's needs?

🎤 **Hints**
ボランティアとしてバングラデシュの地方で働いていることを想像して，自分の考えを書きましょう。

1 Do you know this woman? // Maybe / you have seen her / on TV. // She is Sazae, / the main character / in *Sazae-san*. // *Sazae-san* is one of the most popular animated cartoons / and is loved / by people / of all ages. // It is based on the comic / with the same title / **illustrated** by Machiko Hasegawa. //

5 **2** *Sazae-san* originally appeared / in a local newspaper / in Kyushu / as a series of four-**frame** comics / in 1946. // Each **episode** illustrates Sazae's daily life / with her family members, / friends / and neighbors. //

3 Sazae is a stay-at-home mom / with a two-year-old son / and lives / in her parents' home / with her three-generation family. // She is an energetic and

10 active woman. // She is a little absent-minded / and sometimes makes a lot of mistakes, / but her **cheerfulness** makes people around her happy. //

(127 words)

音読しよう

Practice 1 スラッシュ位置で文を区切って読んでみよう ☐
Practice 2 英語の音の変化に注意して読んでみよう ☐
TRY! 1分15秒以内に本文全体を音読しよう ☐

スピーキング・トレーナー

📖 Reading 本文の内容を読んで理解しよう【知識・技能】【思考力・判断力・表現力】 (共通テスト) (GTEC®)

Make the correct choice to answer each question. (各 5 点 [(3)は完答])

(1) What does "absent-minded" mean in line 10? ☐
　① easygoing　　② forgetful　　③ independent　　④ reliable

(2) According to the passage, what happened in 1946? ☐
　① A local newspaper company began selling comic books of *Sazae-san*.
　② *Sazae-san* originally appeared in a major newspaper in Japan.
　③ *Sazae-san*'s animated cartoons began broadcasting.
　④ Some people living in Kyushu could read *Sazae-san* in their local newspaper.

(3) Which of the following are true? (Choose two options. The order does not matter.)
　☐ · ☐
　① Sazae is a bit careless and sometimes makes mistakes.
　② Sazae is a stay-at-home mom with her two-year-old daughter.
　③ Sazae lives with her husband's parents in a three-generation family.
　④ Sazae's cheerfulness brings smiles to people around her.
　⑤ The *Sazae-san* animated cartoons are more famous and popular than the comics.

🎴 Vocabulary & Grammar　重要表現や文法事項について理解しよう【知識】　(英検®) (GTEC®)

Make the correct choice to complete each sentence.　(各3点)

(1) If I become a cartoonist someday, I would love to (　　　) fantasy stories.
　　① approach　　　　② behave　　　　③ evacuate　　　　④ illustrate

(2) The beautiful picture in the wooden (　　　) is hanging on the wall.
　　① facility　　　　② fertilizer　　　　③ flyer　　　　④ frame

(3) Could you tell me about one of the most exciting (　　　) from your school life?
　　① envelopes　　　　② episodes　　　　③ eruptions　　　　④ explanations

(4) Even in difficult situations, she maintained her (　　　).
　　① cheerfulness　　② communication　　③ construction　　④ hopelessness

(5) Congratulations! I was sure of your (　　　) in the contest.
　　① had succeeded　　② succeed　　③ success　　④ successful

🎧 Listening　英文を聞いて理解しよう【知識・技能】【思考力・判断力・表現力】　(共通テスト) ⊙28

Listen to the English and make the best choice to match the content.　(4点)

　　① One popular singer who is energetic and active is being introduced.
　　② The speaker was a famous actress in the world.
　　③ The well-known actress worked for children as a member of UNICEF.

💬 Interaction　英文を聞いて会話を続けよう【知識・技能】【思考力・判断力・表現力】　スピーキング・トレーナー

Listen to the English and respond to the last remark.　(7点)

〔メ　モ　　　　　　　　　　　　　　　　　　　　　　　　　　　　　　　　　　　　　　　〕

🎧**Hints**
cheer ... up ((人など)を元気づける), encourage (…を励ます), sad and painful (悲しくてつらい)

✍ Production (Writing)　自分の考えを書いて伝えよう【思考力・判断力・表現力】

Write your answer to the following question.　(9点)

Tell me about one of your family members.

🎧**Hints**
家族の年齢や性格について説明しましょう。ペットを飼っている場合は，そのことについて回答しても構いません。

4 In the Showa era, / a "good wife and **wise** mother" / was the ideal image / of Japanese women. // It was thought / that women should be **modest**, / **ladylike**, / and **faithful** / to their husbands. //

5 On the other hand, / Sazae has an equal **relationship** / with her husband, / Masuo. // She is honest / and always expresses her opinions **openly** / and lives her own way. // This is a different image / from that of most Japanese women / at that time. //

6 Machiko Hasegawa once said, / "I want many people / to laugh every day." // She also said, / "If there is a woman / who is always cheerful and honest, / she can motivate those around her / to make the world brighter." // She hoped / many people would lead a happy life, / so she described Sazae / as her ideal image / of a cheerful and honest woman. //

(132 words)

音読しよう　　　　　　　　　　　　　　　　　　スピーキング・トレーナー

Practice 1 スラッシュ位置で文を区切って読んでみよう ☐
Practice 2 英語の音の変化に注意して読んでみよう ☐
TRY! 1分15秒以内に本文全体を音読しよう ☐

Reading　本文の内容を読んで理解しよう【知識・技能】【思考力・判断力・表現力】　　　共通テスト

Make the correct choice to complete each sentence or answer each question. (各5点)

(1) In the Showa era, ☐.

　① a "good wife and wise mother" was already an old image of Japanese women

　② it was thought that women should be faithful to their fathers

　③ people thought that women should be a "good wife and wise mother"

　④ women were more modest than men

(2) Which of the following is **not** true? ☐

　① Sazae always lives her own way.

　② Sazae can express her opinions openly.

　③ Sazae has an equal relationship with her husband.

　④ Sazae is modest and faithful to her husband, Masuo.

(3) Machiko Hasegawa ☐.

　① described Sazae as her ideal image of a cheerful and ladylike woman

　② dreamed that many people would lead a happy life with a smile

　③ hoped many modest women would lead a happy life

　④ thought that Japan would become brighter if there were "good wife and wise mother" figures

💳 Vocabulary & Grammar　重要表現や文法事項について理解しよう【知識】　(英検®) (GTEC®)

Make the correct choice to complete each sentence.　(各3点)

(1) It is said that the new drama is (　　　) to the original work.

① curious　　　② faithful　　　③ same　　　④ significant

(2) The (　　　) old woman is respected in this village.

① wisdom　　　② wise　　　③ wisely　　　④ witness

(3) Her (　　　) attitude gave people around her a good impression.

① discomfort　　　② inaccurate　　　③ modest　　　④ narrow

(4) Finally, Steven (　　　) talked about his mistake to his boss.

① frequently　　　② happily　　　③ openly　　　④ physically

(5) I invited her (　　　) to Osamu's birthday party.

① come　　　② coming　　　③ to be coming　　　④ to come

🎧 Listening　英文を聞いて理解しよう【知識・技能】【思考力・判断力・表現力】　(共通テスト) 💿29

Listen to the English and make the best choice to match the content.　(4点)

① People living in a three-generation family can automatically receive some money.

② The speaker is asking listeners to provide financial support to specific families.

③ The speaker is delivering some information to listeners.

💬 Interaction　英文を聞いて会話を続けよう【知識・技能】【思考力・判断力・表現力】　スピーキング・トレーナー

Listen to the English and respond to the last remark.　(7点)

〔メ モ　　　　　　　　　　　　　　　　　　　　　　　　　　　　　　　　〕

🎧 **Hints**

自分らしく生きるためには何が必要かを考えましょう。

😀 Production (Speaking)　自分の考えを話して伝えよう【思考力・判断力・表現力】　スピーキング・トレーナー

Answer the following question.　(9点)

What type of people do you think easily accept new ideas?　Why?

〔メ モ　　　　　　　　　　　　　　　　　　　　　　　　　　　　　　　　〕

🎧 **Hints**

press one's opinion on ... (…に意見を押しつける)，fixed idea (固定観念)，depend on ... (…次第)

Sazae-san and Machiko Hasegawa

Machiko Hasegawa

1920	She was born / in Saga. // She was a bright and **tomboyish** girl. // She liked drawing pictures. //
1934	She became a private **pupil** / of manga artist / Suihou Tagawa. // At the age of 15, / she made her **debut** / as a manga artist. //
1946	The local newspaper / in Kyushu / asked her / to contribute a series of four-frame comics. // She hit **upon** an idea / that included the main characters / of *Sazae-san* / while walking / on a nearby beach. //
1947	She founded her own publishing company / with her sisters / in order to publish *Sazae-san* herself. //
1969	*Sazae-san* began / as a TV **animation**. //
1992	She passed away / at the age of 72 / and received the People's Honor Award / in the same year. //

Machiko was the first female professional **cartoonist** / in Japan. // She was a strong and independent woman. // Machiko, / as well as Sazae, / was an energetic and active woman / in the Showa era. //

(141 words)

音読しよう   スピーキング・トレーナー

Practice 1 スラッシュ位置で文を区切って読んでみよう ☐
Practice 2 英語の音の変化に注意して読んでみよう ☐
TRY! 1分20秒以内に本文全体を音読しよう ☐

Reading 本文の内容を読んで理解しよう【知識・技能】【思考力・判断力・表現力】   (共通テスト)

Make the correct choice to complete each sentence or answer each question. ((1)は7点, (2)は完答8点)

(1) Before Machiko became a professional cartoonist, ☐.
 ① she entered the school that Suihou Tagawa had established
 ② she hit upon an idea that included the main characters of *Sazae-san*
 ③ she was asked to write a series of four-frame comics for a local newspaper in Kyushu
 ④ she was taught by Suihou Tagawa

(2) Put the following events (①～④) into the order in which they happened.
 ☐ → ☐ → ☐ → ☐
 ① Machiko came up with the idea about *Sazae-san*.
 ② Machiko won the People's Honor Award.
 ③ Machiko started her publishing company with her sisters.
 ④ The TV animation *Sazae-san* began.

Vocabulary & Grammar 重要表現や文法事項について理解しよう【知識】 英検® GTEC®

Make the correct choice to complete each sentence. （各3点）

(1) The interviewer asked the novelist when he hit (　　　) the idea.
　① from　　　② in　　　③ upon　　　④ with

(2) Sally will make her (　　　) as an actress next month.
　① deal　　　② debt　　　③ debut　　　④ doubt

(3) Osamu Tezuka is one of the most famous Japanese (　　　).
　① architects　　② cartoonists　　③ paintings　　④ paints

(4) My teacher told me, "You should be a (　　　) who is a good example to others."
　① manner　　　② moral　　　③ pride　　　④ pupil

(5) While (　　　), you must not use your smartphone.
　① drive　　　② driven　　　③ driving　　　④ drove

Listening 英文を聞いて理解しよう【知識・技能】【思考力・判断力・表現力】 共通テスト 🔊30

Listen to the English and make the best choice to match the content. （4点）

　① Katsuo's younger sister is bright, but absent-minded.
　② Sazae has an older brother named Katsuo.
　③ The speaker is talking about his sister's mistake.

Interaction 英文を聞いて会話を続けよう【知識・技能】【思考力・判断力・表現力】 スピーキング・トレーナー

Listen to the English and respond to the last remark. （7点）

〔メモ　　　　　　　　　　　　　　　　　　　　　　　　　　　　　　　　　　　　　　　〕

🎧 **Hints**
社会に大きな影響を与えたと思う人物をあげ，功績を話してみよう。

Production（Writing） 自分の考えを書いて伝えよう【思考力・判断力・表現力】

Write your answer to the following question. （9点）

In what situations do you hit upon new ideas?

🎧 **Hints**
新しいアイデアはどのようなとき，どのような場所で思いつくか，自分の経験をもとに書いてみよう。

1 Mago Nagasaka, / a street painter, / came across a photo / in 2016. // In the photo, / a child was standing / in a **dump** site overseas. // Shocked by the realities / of the world's waste, / in 2017 / he visited a **slum** / in Ghana / which was described / as the world's largest "**graveyard**" / for electronic devices. //

5 **2** There, / young people were living desperately, / burning the electronic devices / to melt and **extract** the **metals** / inside them. // Those devices had been thrown away / by people / in developed countries / and then dumped / in Ghana. // Many of those young people / breathed in too much **poisonous** gas, / got cancer, / and died / in their thirties. // Mago was **astonished** / to know / that

10 he was leading a comfortable life / at the expense of their lives. //

3 "I'm going to spread this fact / to developed countries / through the power of art," / said Mago. // So, / he started to create artworks / by using electronic waste (e-waste) / **discarded** in Ghana / and sold them. //   (153 words)

🔊 **音読しよう** 📖

Practice 1 スラッシュ位置で文を区切って読んでみよう ☐
Practice 2 英語の音の変化に注意して読んでみよう ☐
TRY! 1分30秒以内に本文全体を音読しよう ☐

スピーキング・トレーナー

📖 **Reading** 本文の内容を読んで理解しよう【知識・技能】【思考力・判断力・表現力】   共通テスト

Make the correct choice to complete each sentence or answer each question. (各5点)

(1) After seeing a photograph, Mago Nagasaka ☐.
  ① decided to become a street painter in a slum in Ghana
  ② described a slum in Ghana as the world's largest "graveyard" in his artworks
  ③ was shocked and went to a slum in Ghana to pick up trash
  ④ was upset and visited a slum in Ghana

(2) Which of the following is true? ☐
  ① Many of the young people in the slum ate poisonous food and got cancer.
  ② Many of the young people in the slum died young.
  ③ Young people in the slum burned electronic devices to extract the money inside them.
  ④ Young people in the slum were leading comfortable lives.

(3) Mago used ☐ for his artworks because he wanted to let the people in the world know a fact in Ghana.
  ① electronic waste   ② some photos in Ghana
  ③ the power of the young people in Ghana ④ too much poisonous gas

Vocabulary & Grammar　重要表現や文法事項について理解しよう【知識】　英検®　GTEC®

Make the correct choice to complete each sentence.　(各3点)

(1)　I came (　　　) a friend from elementary school in front of the station.

　① across　　　② away　　　③ to　　　④ up

(2)　Be careful! Some kinds of snakes around here are (　　　).

　① inaccurate　　② poisonous　　③ solid　　④ steady

(3)　Nick was (　　　) to hear the news that there was a fire in his neighborhood last night.

　① astonished　　② connected　　③ proposed　　④ sneezed

(4)　He (　　　) many clothes in preparation for his move next month.

　① detected　　② devoted　　③ disapproved　　④ discarded

(5)　I was just standing there, (　　　) what to do.

　① didn't know　　② not know　　③ not knowing　　④ not known

Listening　英文を聞いて理解しよう【知識・技能】【思考力・判断力・表現力】　共通テスト　31

Listen to the English and make the best choice to match the content.　(4点)

　① Some children in developing countries use used equipment from developed countries.

　② Tablets and PCs are imported from developed countries to developing countries.

　③ The speaker complains about the current recycling system.

Interaction　英文を聞いて会話を続けよう【知識・技能】【思考力・判断力・表現力】　スピーキング・トレーナー

Listen to the English and respond to the last remark.　(7点)

〔メモ〕

🎧**Hints**

chocolate (チョコレート)，West Africa (西アフリカ)，Côte d'Ivoire (コートジボワール)

Production (Writing)　自分の考えを書いて伝えよう【思考力・判断力・表現力】

Write your answer to the following question.　(9点)

What kind of waste problems do you think Japan has?

🎧**Hints**

separate (…を分別する)，disposal (処分)，pick up ... (…を拾う)，burnable (可燃性の)

4 Mago believes / that sustainable **economic growth** is important. // So, / he has used the profits / from his artworks / to promote it / from the following perspectives: / education, culture and economy. //

5 In 2018, / Mago started the first school / in the slum, / "MAGO ART AND STUDY." // It will be free / to attend / as long as Mago lives. // Children learn subjects / like English and arithmetic / there. //

6 In August 2019, / Mago founded the "MAGO E-Waste Museum," / the first cultural facility / in the slums. // He believes / that the museum will help / to bring culture and new jobs, / and **foster** a **hopeful** new society. //

7 Mago has set his sights / on building a state-of-the-art recycling plant / in Ghana. // He is going to **hire** people / from the slums / to work / in his factory. // That way, / **none** of the local people / will need to do dangerous work / at the risk of their health. // Mago hopes / to turn the graveyard of e-waste / into a zero-pollution sustainable town. //

(155 words)

音読しよう 📖

スピーキング・トレーナー

Practice 1 スラッシュ位置で文を区切って読んでみよう ☐
Practice 2 英語の音の変化に注意して読んでみよう ☐
TRY! 1分30秒以内に本文全体を音読しよう ☐

Reading 本文の内容を読んで理解しよう【知識・技能】【思考力・判断力・表現力】

共通テスト GTEC®

Make the correct choice to complete each sentence or answer each question. (各5点)

(1) What does "perspective" mean in line 3? ☐
① degree   ② impression   ③ scenery   ④ viewpoint

(2) Which of the following is **not** true? ☐
① Mago established the first school in the slum in 2018.
② Mago thinks "MAGO E-Waste Museum" can make the slums hopeful societies.
③ Mago tried to encourage economic growth in Ghana using the profits from his artworks.
④ The children in the slum can learn English and arithmetic at the "MAGO E-Waste Museum."

(3) One **opinion** from the article is that ☐.
① "MAGO ART AND STUDY" is the first school in the slum
② Mago has used the profits from his artworks to promote the slums' economic growth
③ Mago plans to employ people from the slums in his factory
④ the "MAGO E-Waste Museum" will help to bring culture and new jobs to the slums

Vocabulary & Grammar 重要表現や文法事項について理解しよう【知識】 (英検®) (GTEC®)

Make the correct choice to complete each sentence. (各3点)

(1) ( ) there is a chance, I would like to keep trying.
　① As long as　　② As possible as　　③ As soon as　　④ As well as

(2) You can sell the books and ( ) them into cash at the second-hand shop.
　① charge　　② pay　　③ take　　④ turn

(3) The agreement will ( ) stronger relations between the two countries.
　① brighten　　② foster　　③ invent　　④ register

(4) Since he was not good at housework, he ( ) a housekeeper.
　① commanded　　② hired　　③ instructed　　④ organized

(5) Unfortunately, ( ) of the furniture in the store was attractive.
　① no　　② none　　③ not　　④ nothing

Listening 英文を聞いて理解しよう【知識・技能】【思考力・判断力・表現力】 (共通テスト) 32

Listen to the English and make the best choice to match the content. (4点)

　① Ghana is still famous for its cacao and gold production.
　② Ghana is the world's top producer of cacao.
　③ The speaker says that there used to be a lot of gold in Ghana.

Interaction 英文を聞いて会話を続けよう【知識・技能】【思考力・判断力・表現力】 スピーキング・トレーナー

Listen to the English and respond to the last remark. (7点)

〔メモ 　　　　　　　　　　　　　　　　　　　　　　　　　　　　　　　　　〕

Hints
workplace accident (労働災害), well-organized (整理整頓された), assume (…だと仮定する), measure (対策)

Production (Speaking) 自分の考えを話して伝えよう【思考力・判断力・表現力】 スピーキング・トレーナー

Answer the following question. (9点)

Imagine that you want to start a big project which needs a lot of money. How would you secure enough funds?

〔メモ 　　　　　　　　　　　　　　　　　　　　　　　　　　　　　　　　　〕

Hints
fund (資金), subsidy (補助金), sponsor (スポンサー), make a loan (借金する)

Kumi : What do you think / about the e-waste problem? //

Takashi : New smartphones and **tablets** / are released / one after another. // They look very attractive. // But / we have to think twice / before buying a new device. // We should ask ourselves / if we really need a new one. //

5 *Kumi :* I agree with you, / Takashi. // In addition, / once we've got a device, / we have to use it / until it no longer works. // We have to treat it / with care. // It's also important / to repair and reuse our devices. //

Vivian : Exactly. // We consumers should become more aware / of the e-waste problem. // Also, / I think / the **manufacturers** should be responsible / for

10 **disposal** of their products / when they are no longer **usable**. //

Takashi : You have a good point! // Governments should require the manufacturers / to collect e-waste / by setting up collection centers / or take-back systems, / either **individually** or **collectively**. //

Kumi : Great. //

(137 words)

音読しよう

スピーキング・トレーナー

Practice 1 スラッシュ位置で文を区切って読んでみよう ☐
Practice 2 英語の音の変化に注意して読んでみよう ☐
TRY! 1分20秒以内に本文全体を音読しよう ☐

Reading 本文の内容を読んで理解しよう【知識・技能】【思考力・判断力・表現力】 共通テスト

Make the correct choice to complete each sentence or answer each question. (各5点)

(1) Who starts to talk about the need for fixing devices? ☐
　① Kumi 　　　② None of them 　　③ Takashi 　　④ Vivian

(2) One of Vivian's opinions is that ☐.
　① consumers should think twice before buying new items
　② consumers should take the issue of the e-waste more seriously
　③ manufacturers are more aware of the e-waste problem than consumers
　④ manufacturers should release new products one after another

(3) Which of the following is **not** true? ☐
　① Kumi agrees with all of Takashi's opinions.
　② Takashi believes that consumers should consider whether they truly need a new product.
　③ Takashi understands that new products look very attractive.
　④ Vivian thinks that governments should require the manufacturers to collect e-waste.

💳 Vocabulary & Grammar　重要表現や文法事項について理解しよう【知識】　英検® GTEC®

Make the correct choice to complete each sentence.　(各3点)

(1)　We need to think (　　　) before making a big decision.
　① many　　　　　② once　　　　　③ second　　　　　④ twice

(2)　The (　　　) size of the mailbox is limited.
　① usable　　　　② use　　　　　③ useful　　　　　④ using

(3)　The committee decided to continue to discuss the (　　　) of nuclear waste.
　① dialect　　　　② disease　　　　③ disposal　　　　④ diverse

(4)　I decided to talk to each team member (　　　).
　① accidentally　② collectively　③ individually　④ strangely

(5)　Do you know (　　　) David will attend the meeting tomorrow?
　① if　　　　　　② unless　　　　③ until　　　　　④ while

🎧 Listening　英文を聞いて理解しよう【知識・技能】【思考力・判断力・表現力】　共通テスト　💿 33

Listen to the English and make the best choice to match the content.　(4点)

　① Consumers may pay more for new products.
　② Manufacturers should be responsible for disposal at no additional cost.
　③ The speaker says that consumers should be more aware of waste disposal.

💬 Interaction　英文を聞いて会話を続けよう【知識・技能】【思考力・判断力・表現力】　スピーキング・トレーナー

Listen to the English and respond to the last remark.　(7点)

〔メモ　　　　　　　　　　　　　　　　　　　　　　　　　　　　　　　　　　　　　　　〕

🎺 **Hints**
最新のスマートフォンを持ちたい理由を話してみよう。持ちたくない人は，持ちたい人の気持ちを想像して答えてみよう。

✍ Production (Writing)　自分の考えを書いて伝えよう【思考力・判断力・表現力】

Write your answer to the following question.　(9点)

Explain the items that you are reusing or intend to reuse.

🎺 **Hints**
再利用の取り組みについて書いてみましょう。

1 Iceland is a Nordic island country / located in the North Atlantic Ocean, / with a population of about 350,000. // The country has been **ranked** first / in **gender equality** / by the World Economic **Forum** / for over ten years. // How are women playing an active role / in Icelandic society? //

5 **2** In Iceland, / more women are active / in **politics** / than in many other countries. // About 40% / of the members / of **parliament** / are women. // Women have a major influence / on policy making / **regarding** welfare, / education / and **wages**. //

3 In addition, / the employment **rate** / of women in Iceland / is higher / than 80%. // There is a good working environment / for women, / and many working 10 mothers take their babies / to work / with them. // The childcare leave system / is well developed, / and a high percentage / of men / as well as women / take childcare leave. // Many companies are also trying / to eliminate the wage gap / between men and women. // Iceland may be the best place / in the world / for working women / who have children. //

(162 words)

🔊 **音読しよう** 📖　～～～～～～～～～　スピーキング・トレーナー

Practice 1 スラッシュ位置で文を区切って読んでみよう ☐
Practice 2 英語の音の変化に注意して読んでみよう ☐
TRY! 1分35秒以内に本文全体を音読しよう ☐

📖 **Reading** 本文の内容を読んで理解しよう【知識・技能】【思考力・判断力・表現力】　共通テスト　GTEC®

Make the correct choice to complete each sentence or answer each question. (各5点)

(1) What does "wage" mean in line 7? ☐
　① economy　　　② pay　　　③ society　　　④ well-being

(2) In Iceland, women ☐.
　① are playing an active role in politics
　② earn more money than men
　③ have a major influence on policy making regarding welfare, education and the military
　④ work longer and harder than those in other countries

(3) One **fact** from the article is that ☐.
　① Iceland may be the best place in the world for working women who have children
　② many working mothers take their babies to work with them
　③ the childcare leave system is well developed, and a high percentage of men take it
　④ there is a good working environment for women in Iceland

Vocabulary & Grammar 重要表現や文法事項について理解しよう【知識】　英検® GTEC®

Make the correct choice to complete each sentence.　（各3点）

(1)　*A:* May I take (　　　) next Monday?　*B:* Of course, you can.
　　① after　　　　　② apart　　　　　③ care of　　　　　④ leave

(2)　In some Western countries, many people have fought for (　　　) and human rights.
　　① emergency　　② equality　　　　③ evacuation　　　④ explanation

(3)　Please contact us if you have any questions (　　　) the product.
　　① according　　② belonging　　　③ expecting　　　④ regarding

(4)　The CEO announced a decision to increase the (　　　) level for factory workers.
　　① bill　　　　　② charge　　　　　③ coin　　　　　　④ wage

(5)　*A:* This bag is a little small for a one-day trip.
　　B: Why don't you use a (　　　) one?
　　① big　　　　　② bigger　　　　　③ bigger than　　　④ biggest of

🎧 Listening 英文を聞いて理解しよう【知識・技能】【思考力・判断力・表現力】　共通テスト ◉34

Listen to the English and make the best choice to match the content.　（4点）
　　① Gender equality in the workplace is a topic that needs to be reconsidered.
　　② Many companies require all their employees to clean the offices themselves.
　　③ There is a large wage gap between men and women in Japan.

💬 Interaction 英文を聞いて会話を続けよう【知識・技能】【思考力・判断力・表現力】　スピーキング・トレーナー

Listen to the English and respond to the last remark.　（7点）
　〔メモ　　　　　　　　　　　　　　　　　　　　　　　　　　　　　　　　　　　　〕

> **Hints**
> 学校における，男女で違うものについて答えましょう。今の時代の話でも，昔の時代の話でも構いません。

✍ Production (Writing) 自分の考えを書いて伝えよう【思考力・判断力・表現力】

Write your answer to the following question.　（9点）
Explain one thing you know about Iceland.

> **Hints**
> the North Atlantic Ocean (北大西洋)，glacier (氷河)，volcano (火山)，aurora (オーロラ)

To Achieve Gender Equality

4 How has Iceland achieved gender equality? // In Iceland, / it used to be common / for women / to do housework and childcare / as full-time **housewives**. // Even if they were working, / women's **income** was much lower / than men's. // Women felt **dissatisfied** / with such a situation. //

5 **5** On October 24, / 1975, / about 90% / of adult females / in Iceland / went on **strike** / to **protest** against gender **inequality** / in their workplaces and families. // On that day, / they **boycotted** all their work and housework, / and gathered together / in a square / in the capital city, / Reykjavik. // The strike made the men realize / that they could not live a single day / without women. //

10 **6** As a result of the strike, / Icelandic society started to change. // In 1980, / the first female president / was **elected**. // Social **institutions** and laws / for gender equality / were developed. // The working conditions / for women / also improved, / and the wage gap was gradually reduced. // These movements / toward gender equality / succeeded in making Iceland what it is now. //

(158 words)

音読しよう

Practice 1 スラッシュ位置で文を区切って読んでみよう ☐
Practice 2 英語の音の変化に注意して読んでみよう ☐
TRY! 1分30秒以内に本文全体を音読しよう ☐

スピーキング・トレーナー

Reading 本文の内容を読んで理解しよう【知識・技能】【思考力・判断力・表現力】　共通テスト GTEC®

Make the correct choice to answer each question. （各5点 [(3)は完答]）

(1) What does "achieve" mean in line 1? ☐
　① acknowledge　② notice　③ realize　④ rely

(2) Which of the following is **not** true? ☐
　① A lot of women stopped working and doing house chores on the day of the boycott.
　② About 90% of adult males and females in Iceland went on strike.
　③ Before the boycott, women were often paid less than men in Iceland.
　④ The strike in Iceland changed mens' thinking.

(3) After the strike, what happened to Icelandic society? (Choose two options. The order does not matter.) ☐ · ☐
　① Many women were forced to do housework and childcare as full-time housewives.
　② Social systems and laws for gender equality were developed.
　③ The first female queen was elected.
　④ The government made women work harder than before.
　⑤ The wage gap decreased little by little.

Vocabulary & Grammar　重要表現や文法事項について理解しよう【知識】　英検® GTEC®

Make the correct choice to complete each sentence.　（各3点）

(1) Eric stayed at a luxury hotel but was (　　　) with the service.
　　① delighted　　　　② dissatisfied　　　③ excited　　　　④ grateful

(2) After changing jobs, my (　　　) increased significantly.
　　① incident　　　　② income　　　　③ outbreak　　　④ outcome

(3) Ellie was (　　　) class president by a vote.
　　① devoted　　　　② divided　　　　③ elected　　　④ involved

(4) The citizens gathered in the streets to (　　　) against unfair government policies.
　　① apologize　　　② approve　　　　③ ensure　　　④ protest

(5) Kate often says, "Speaking Japanese is (　　　) easier than writing it."
　　① a lot of　　　　② far　　　　　③ more　　　④ very

Listening　英文を聞いて理解しよう【知識・技能】【思考力・判断力・表現力】　共通テスト　🔘35

Listen to the English and make the best choice to match the content.　（4点）
　① The speaker is explaining one of the human rights that workers have.
　② The speaker joined a strike yesterday.
　③ There was a strike demanding higher wages yesterday.

Interaction　英文を聞いて会話を続けよう【知識・技能】【思考力・判断力・表現力】　スピーキング・トレーナー

Listen to the English and respond to the last remark.　（7点）
〔メモ　　　　　　　　　　　　　　　　　　　　　　　　　　　　　　　　　　　〕

🎧 Hints
男女平等が実現したら，今とはどのように変わるか考えてみましょう。

Production (Speaking)　自分の考えを話して伝えよう【思考力・判断力・表現力】　スピーキング・トレーナー

Answer the following question.　（9点）

What do you think are the disadvantages of going on strike?
〔メモ　　　　　　　　　　　　　　　　　　　　　　　　　　　　　　　　　　　〕

🎧 Hints
no work, no pay（働かなければ賃金は支払われない，とする原則），illegal（違法の），discharge（…を解雇する）

Japan 120th / in Global Gender Equality **Ranking** //

Japan has one of the highest gender inequality rates / in the world. // In the World Economic Forum's Global Gender Equality Ranking / in 2021, / Japan's **scorecard** was 120 / out of 156 countries. // This ranking was the lowest / of
5 the G7 countries. // On the other hand, / Nordic countries, / including Iceland, / were at the top of the list. //

Why does Japan have such a low ranking? // In the Global Gender Equality Ranking, / gender **disparity** is **quantified** and **evaluated** / in four areas: / politics, / **economics**, / education / and health. // The gender gap / in Japan /
10 is **particularly** large, / especially in the **political** and economic fields. // The **involvement** of women / in these fields / is an **urgent** issue. //

The Japanese government is trying / to encourage gender equality / but we are not succeeding / in achieving it. // We should learn / from Nordic countries / and try to change deeply rooted social practices. // We must have a clear goal /
15 — to create a better working environment / for both women and men / — and make **continuous** efforts / to realize it / for ourselves. //

(166 words)

音読しよう　　　　　　　　　　　　　　　　　　　　スピーキング・トレーナー

Practice 1 スラッシュ位置で文を区切って読んでみよう ☐
Practice 2 英語の音の変化に注意して読んでみよう ☐
TRY! 1分35秒以内に本文全体を音読しよう ☐

📖 Reading　本文の内容を読んで理解しよう【知識・技能】【思考力・判断力・表現力】　　　(共通テスト)(GTEC®)

Make the correct choice to complete each sentence or answer each question. (各5点)

(1) What does "practice" mean in line 14? ☐
　① attempt　　　　② custom　　　　③ document　　　　④ knowledge

(2) Which of the following is true? ☐
　① Japan ranked the lowest in the Global Gender Equality Ranking in 2021.
　② Many Nordic countries have achieved gender equality more successfully than other countries.
　③ The gender gap in Japan in education and economic fields is not large.
　④ The number of Japanese women involved in political and economic fields is decreasing.

(3) One **fact** from the article is that ☐ .
　① Japan ranked the lowest among the G7 countries in the Global Gender Equality Ranking in 2021
　② Japanese women should be involved especially in the political and economic fields
　③ we must make continuous efforts to realize gender equality for ourselves
　④ we should learn gender equality from Nordic countries

Goals

🔊英語の音の変化を理解して音読することができる。 📖男女平等ランキングに関する新聞記事を読んで概要や要点をとらえることができる。
📝文脈を理解して適切な語句を用いて英文を完成することができる。 🎧平易な英語で話される短い英文を聞いて必要な情報を聞き取ることができる。
💬日本とアイスランドの共通点について簡単な語句を用いて情報や考えを伝えることができる。 ✍男女不平等の問題について簡単な語句を用いて考えを表現することができる。

🔖 Vocabulary & Grammar 重要表現や文法事項について理解しよう【知識】 英検® GTEC®

Make the correct choice to complete each sentence. （各3点）

(1) In this year's competition, Japanese players were at the (　　　) of the rankings.
　　① name　　　　② power　　　　③ quality　　　　④ top

(2) In the dance contest, both performance and teamwork are (　　　).
　　① calculated　　② evacuated　　③ evaluated　　④ indicated

(3) News reports say that there will be a (　　　) conflict between the two parties.
　　① pleasant　　② polite　　③ political　　④ precious

(4) I received an (　　　) call for help from Beth.
　　① artificial　　② entire　　③ opposite　　④ urgent

(5) Due to heavy traffic, it will take at (　　　) an hour to reach the airport.
　　① best　　　　② first　　　　③ last　　　　④ least

🎧 Listening 英文を聞いて理解しよう【知識・技能】【思考力・判断力・表現力】 共通テスト 💿36

Listen to the English and make the best choice to match the content. （4点）

　① In Iceland, parents are attempting to obtain the right to take paid leave.
　② Japanese parents have trouble taking a day off when their children are sick.
　③ The speaker would like to take paid leave because his child has become sick.

💬 Interaction 英文を聞いて会話を続けよう【知識・技能】【思考力・判断力・表現力】 スピーキング・トレーナー

Listen to the English and respond to the last remark. （7点）

　〔メモ　　　　　　　　　　　　　　　　　　　　　　　　　　　　　　　　　〕

🎧 **Hints**
　island country (島国)，volcano (火山)，hot spring (温泉)，earthquake (地震)，the fishing industry (漁業)

✍ Production（Writing） 自分の考えを書いて伝えよう【思考力・判断力・表現力】

Write your answer to the following question. （9点）

What issues do you think exist regarding gender inequality in the world?　Refer to SDG Goal 5.

🎧 **Hints**
　SDGs の目標5「ジェンダー平等を実現しよう」を参考に，世界にはどのような男女不平等の問題があるか考えましょう。

Part 3　71

Imagine an ocean / without fish. // Imagine your meals / without any seafood. // This is the future / if we do not think seriously / and act soon. //

This is the message / which the film / titled *The End of the Line* / gives us. // The film is the world's first major **documentary** / to focus on the impact / of
5 **overfishing** / on the world's oceans. // Scientists predict / that if we continue to fish / as we are doing now, / we will see the end / of most seafood / by 2048. //

The film **highlights** / how many well-known species / are likely to die out. // For example, / **bluefin** tuna are among them. // In Spain, / the catch of bluefin tuna / has **exponentially** decreased: / 5,000 million tons / in 1999, / 2,000 million
10 tons / in 2000, / and 900 million tons / in 2005. // However, / they are still being caught **excessively** / because of the increasing demand / for sushi / in Western countries. // The film **implies** / that a world with no fish / will experience **mass starvation**. //

(156 words)

🗣)) 音読しよう 📖 〜〜〜〜〜〜〜〜〜〜〜〜〜〜〜〜 スピーキング・トレーナー

Practice 1 スラッシュ位置で文を区切って読んでみよう ☐
Practice 2 音声を聞きながら，音声のすぐ後を追って読んでみよう ☐
TRY! 1分25秒以内に本文全体を音読しよう ☐

📖 **Reading** 本文の内容を読んで理解しよう【知識・技能】【思考力・判断力・表現力】 共通テスト GTEC®

Make the correct choice to complete each sentence or answer each question. (各5点)

(1) What does "impact" mean in line 4? ☐
　① applause　　　② influence　　　③ request　　　④ resistance

(2) The film titled *The End of the Line* ☐ .
　① emphasizes that many famous species are in danger of extinction
　② shows that the catch of bluefin tuna has gradually decreased
　③ stresses that the demand for sushi in Western countries is growing
　④ was made by many scientists around the world

(3) If we do not think seriously about the problems that are happening in the oceans, ☐ .
　① the catch of bluefin tuna in Spain will increase
　② there will be no fish in the world's oceans by 2048
　③ we may experience mass starvation in a world with no fish
　④ we will receive some messages from the film

Goals

🔊 意味の区切りを理解してスムーズに音読することができる。　📖 魚の乱獲に関する英文を読んで概要や要点をとらえることができる。
✍ 文脈を理解して適切な語句を用いて英文を完成することができる。　🎧 平易な英語で話される短い英文を聞いて必要な情報を聞き取ることができる。
💬 魚がいない世界について簡単な語句を用いて情報や考えを伝えることができる。　✍ 捕鯨の是非について簡単な語句を用いて考えを表現することができる。

🗂 Vocabulary & Grammar　重要表現や文法事項について理解しよう【知識】　英検®　GTEC®

Make the correct choice to complete each sentence.　（各3点）

(1) According to the research, these birds may soon die (　　　).
　① down　　　　　② from　　　　　③ of　　　　　④ out

(2) The teacher (　　　) the last part of the paragraph because it was very important.
　① highlighted　　② ignored　　　③ knocked　　　④ released

(3) The restaurant received a negative review that the prices were (　　　) high compared to the quality of the dishes.
　① efficiently　　② evenly　　　③ eventually　　④ excessively

(4) The government should have secured enough food to avoid (　　　).
　① stability　　　② starvation　　③ structure　　　④ survival

(5) I have to commute to school by bus because my bicycle is (　　　).
　① being repaired　② being repairing　③ repaired　　④ repairing

🎧 Listening　英文を聞いて理解しよう【知識・技能】【思考力・判断力・表現力】　共通テスト　💿37

Listen to the English and make the best choice to match the content.　（4点）

　① Listeners will get the supplement for free by calling the company immediately.
　② The speaker is recommending the supplement.
　③ The supplement has all kinds of nutrition.

💬 Interaction　英文を聞いて会話を続けよう【知識・技能】【思考力・判断力・表現力】　スピーキング・トレーナー

Listen to the English and respond to the last remark.　（7点）

〔メモ　　　　　　　　　　　　　　　　　　　　　　　　　　　　　　　　〕

🎧 **Hints**
魚がいない世界を想像して答えましょう。

✍ Production (Writing)　自分の考えを書いて伝えよう【思考力・判断力・表現力】

Write your answer to the following question.　（9点）

Should we stop hunting and eating whales?　Why?

🎧 **Hints**
whale fishing (捕鯨), anti-whaling (捕鯨に反対の), illegal (違法な), cruel (残酷な)

Fishing with modern technology / is one of the most **destructive** activities / on earth. // **Trawling**, / in **particular**, / is very harmful. // To understand / how harmful it actually is, / let's compare trawling / for fish / in the ocean / to carrying out the same practice / on land. // Imagine a huge net / **sweeping**
5 across the **plains** / of Africa / and catching lions, / elephants / and **rhinos**. // It also pulls out every plant and tree. //

Such destructive activity / is carried out / every day / in every sea and ocean / across the world. // People, / however, / pay little attention / to what is happening / under the sea / because it is **invisible**. //

10 Technology in the fishing industry / has advanced. // **Ironically**, / however, / this has contributed to overfishing. // The Global **Positioning** System / and **sonars** / are used / in fish **finders**. // They can find the locations / of a **shoal** of fish **underwater**, / give information / about their **quantity**, / and even make three-**dimensional** images. // Fishing boats are now **equipped** / with improved engines,
15 nets and lines. //

(155 words)

音読しよう   スピーキング・トレーナー

Practice 1 スラッシュ位置で文を区切って読んでみよう ☐
Practice 2 音声を聞きながら，音声のすぐ後を追って読んでみよう ☐
TRY! 1分20秒以内に本文全体を音読しよう ☐

Reading   本文の内容を読んで理解しよう【知識・技能】【思考力・判断力・表現力】   共通テスト

Make the correct choice to complete each sentence or answer each question.   ((1)は7点, (2)は8点)

(1) ☐☐☐☐ , people don't care much about the problems regarding the ocean.
   ① Because they cannot see what is happening in the sea
   ② Because they have already known that modern fishing technology is the most destructive activities
   ③ Since the catching on land is more destructive than that in the sea
   ④ Since trawling is a destructive activity occurring every day in the ocean

(2) Which of the following is **not** true? ☐☐☐☐
   ① Fish finders can tell you information about the quality of a shoal of fish underwater.
   ② Fish finders use the Global Positioning System and sonars.
   ③ Fishing boats are equipped with high-performance engines, nets and lines.
   ④ Technology in the fishing industry has advanced and caused overfishing.

Vocabulary & Grammar 重要表現や文法事項について理解しよう【知識】 (英検®) (GTEC®)

Make the correct choice to complete each sentence. （各3点）

(1) A team composed of some experts will carry (　　　) a field survey next month.
　① away　　　　② off　　　　③ out　　　　④ over

(2) This new car is (　　　) with small sensors for safety.
　① enable　　　② equipped　　③ exploded　　④ exposed

(3) The magician performed a wonderful trick in which he made himself (　　　) to the audience.
　① accessible　② affordable　③ invisible　　④ uncomfortable

(4) The wine contains large (　　　) of alcohol.
　① depths　　　② heights　　　③ quantities　　④ materials

(5) I have very (　　　) confidence to try it because I am so afraid of failing.
　① least　　　　② less　　　　③ lessen　　　④ little

Listening 英文を聞いて理解しよう【知識・技能】【思考力・判断力・表現力】 (共通テスト) 🎙38

Listen to the English and make the best choice to match the content. （4点）
　① The speaker is giving an example of the problems of overfishing.
　② The speaker says that the target fish were smaller than he expected.
　③ The speaker thinks bycatch is better than overfishing.

Interaction 英文を聞いて会話を続けよう【知識・技能】【思考力・判断力・表現力】 スピーキング・トレーナー

Listen to the English and respond to the remarks. （7点）
〔メ モ　　　　　　　　　　　　　　　　　　　　　　　　　　　　　　　　　　　　〕
🎙 **Hints**
海で起こっている問題に注目させるにはどうすればよいか考えましょう。

Production (Speaking) 自分の考えを話して伝えよう【思考力・判断力・表現力】 スピーキング・トレーナー

Answer the following question. （9点）
What measures do you think should be taken to prevent overfishing?
〔メ モ　　　　　　　　　　　　　　　　　　　　　　　　　　　　　　　　　　　　〕
🎙 **Hints**
restrict (…を制限する)，impose (…を課する)，regulate (…を規制する)

Who is responsible / for the situation? // Consumers buy endangered fish / without thinking about the impact / on the environment. // **Politicians ignore** the advice and warnings / from scientists. // Fishermen break **quotas** / and fish illegally. // The global fishing industry / is slow to **react** / to the disaster / so

5 near at hand. //

The documentary / *The End of the Line* / shows simple and possible solutions / for this international problem. // Every country needs to control fishing / by reducing the number / of fishing boats / across the world. // We should protect large areas / of the ocean / as **marine reserves**. // Consumers should buy fish /

10 only from **certified** sustainable **fisheries**. //

"Overfishing is one of the great environmental disasters," / said one of the film producers. // "I hope / the film will change our lifestyles / and what we eat." // Charles Clover, / the **author** of the book / which the film is based on, / says, / "We must act now / to protect the sea / from overfishing / in order to pass rich

15 marine resources / to the next generation." // (160 words)

🔊)) **音読しよう** 📖 ━━━━━━━━━━━━━━ **スピーキング・トレーナー**

Practice 1 スラッシュ位置で文を区切って読んでみよう ☐
Practice 2 音声を聞きながら，音声のすぐ後を追って読んでみよう ☐
TRY! 1分25秒以内に本文全体を音読しよう ☐

📖 **Reading** 本文の内容を読んで理解しよう【知識・技能】【思考力・判断力・表現力】 共通テスト GTEC®

Make the correct choice to complete each sentence or answer each question. （各5点）

(1) What does "warning" mean in line 3? ☐
　① attention ② caution ③ foundation ④ intention

(2) Which of the following is **not** true? ☐
　① Consumers should choose fish from certified sustainable fisheries.
　② Every country needs to reduce the number of fishermen and control fishing.
　③ Large areas of the ocean must be preserved as marine reserves.
　④ We can learn solutions for the problem from *The End of the Line*.

(3) One **fact** from the article is that ☐.
　① Charles Clover is the author of the book on which the film is based
　② overfishing is one of the major environmental destructions
　③ *The End of the Line* will change our lifestyles and what we eat
　④ we must take action to protect the sea from overfishing

🎴 Vocabulary & Grammar 　重要表現や文法事項について理解しよう【知識】 　英検® 　GTEC®

Make the correct choice to complete each sentence. （各3点）

(1) The company surveys consumers about how they (　　　) to their new product.

① react　　　　　② reflect　　　　　③ repeat　　　　　④ respect

(2) No matter how much Betty tried to get his attention, he (　　　) her.

① ignored　　　　② infected　　　　③ informed　　　　④ invented

(3) Does this restaurant serve (　　　) organic meat?

① accepted　　　② agreed　　　　　③ certified　　　　④ potential

(4) The (　　　) of *Snow Country* is Yasunari Kawabata.

① activist　　　　② architect　　　　③ artist　　　　　④ author

(5) (　　　) you need is a clear vision and determination to achieve your goals.

① How　　　　　② What　　　　　③ When　　　　　④ Which

🎧 Listening 　英文を聞いて理解しよう【知識・技能】【思考力・判断力・表現力】 　共通テスト　💿39

Listen to the English and make the best choice to match the content. （4点）

① ABC Supermarket is making an effort to protect the marine environment.

② The speaker is recommending an MSC-labeled product.

③ There are no MSC-labeled products in stock at ABC Supermarket.

💬 Interaction 　英文を聞いて会話を続けよう【知識・技能】【思考力・判断力・表現力】 　スピーキング・トレーナー

Listen to the English and respond to the last remark. （7点）

〔メモ 　　　　　　　　　　　　　　　　　　　　　　　　　　　　　　　　　　　　　　　〕

🎧 **Hints**

water temperature (水温)，ocean current (海流)，tropical fish (熱帯魚)，plankton (プランクトン)

✍️ Production (Writing) 　自分の考えを書いて伝えよう【思考力・判断力・表現力】

Write your answer to the following question. （9点）

What is the role of the ocean?　Explain its benefits other than providing marine resources.

🎧 **Hints**

海には，水産資源を提供する以外にどのような役割があるか考えましょう。

Lesson 16 A World with No Fish

Does the film affect / consumer attitudes and **intentions**? //

A survey was **conducted** / before and after the film's **premiere** / in theaters. // Before watching the film, / 26% of these audiences **indicated** / that they did not believe overfishing / to be a serious problem. // What happened / to this group /
5 after watching the film? // Eighty-five percent of them answered / that it was quite a big problem. //

The audiences were also asked / about their buying habits / before the film / and their intended buying habits / after the film. // The percentage of the audiences / who had the intention / to buy only sustainable fish / almost doubled /
10 from 43% / to 84%. //

The impact was even more **profound** / on the group / who were not aware of the problems / of overfishing. // Only 17% of this group / bought sustainable fish / before watching the film. // However, / after watching, / 82% said / they would now try / to buy sustainable fish. // (144 words)

🔊)) **音読しよう** 📖 〜〜〜〜〜〜〜〜〜〜〜〜〜〜〜〜〜〜〜〜 スピーキング・トレーナー

Practice 1 スラッシュ位置で文を区切って読んでみよう ☐
Practice 2 音声を聞きながら，音声のすぐ後を追って読んでみよう ☐
TRY! 1分15秒以内に本文全体を音読しよう ☐

📖 Reading 本文の内容を読んで理解しよう【知識・技能】【思考力・判断力・表現力】 (共通テスト)

Make the correct choice to complete each sentence or answer each question. ((1)は7点, (2)は8点)

(1) Which of the following is true? ☐
　① After watching the film, a lot of audiences changed their thinking.
　② Before watching the film, most of the audiences didn't know about overfishing at all.
　③ Half of the audiences thought overfishing was a big problem before watching the film.
　④ The percentage of the audiences' intention to buy only sustainable fish was reduced by half.

(2) After watching the film, ☐.
　① eighty-five percent of the audiences answered overfishing is not a serious problem
　② many people who had not considered the problems of overfishing said they would try to buy sustainable fish
　③ the audiences were asked about their buying habits
　④ the percentage of people with the intention to buy only sustainable fish has decreased from 84% to 43%

Goals

🔊意味の区切りを理解してスムーズに音読することができる。　📖映画に関する報告書を読んで概要や要点をとらえることができる。
📝文脈を理解して適切な語句を用いて英文を完成することができる。　🎧平易な英語で話される短い英文を聞いて必要な情報を聞き取ることができる。
💬環境問題への意識の変化について簡単な語句を用いて情報や考えを伝えることができる。　🗣海の環境を守るためにできることについて簡単な語句を用いて考えを表現することができる。

🎴 Vocabulary & Grammar　重要表現や文法事項について理解しよう【知識】　英検® GTEC®

Make the correct choice to complete each sentence.　（各3点）

(1) Tom has the (　　　　) to start his own business and become an entrepreneur.
　　① injury　　　　　② insight　　　　　③ instrument　　　　④ intention

(2) The police (　　　　) a thorough investigation to gather evidence and solved the crime.
　　① competed　　　　② conducted　　　　③ consumed　　　　④ contained

(3) There are (　　　　) differences in the development of energy resources between the two countries.
　　① painful　　　　　② precious　　　　　③ profound　　　　④ promising

(4) The latest data (　　　　) method will be introduced by some experts at the next conference.
　　① analysis　　　　② analysts　　　　　③ analyze　　　　④ angle

(5) We consider her (　　　　) an excellent leader for the new project.
　　① being　　　　　② is　　　　　　　③ to be　　　　　④ will be

🎧 Listening　英文を聞いて理解しよう【知識・技能】【思考力・判断力・表現力】　共通テスト 🔘40

Listen to the English and make the best choice to match the content.　（4点）

　① According to the survey, young people don't like to eat fish.
　② Many people prefer boneless meat to boneless fish.
　③ The study shows how the number of people who like to eat fish has changed.

💬 Interaction　英文を聞いて会話を続けよう【知識・技能】【思考力・判断力・表現力】　スピーキング・トレーナー

Listen to the English and respond to the last remark.　（7点）

〔メ モ　　　　　　　　　　　　　　　　　　　　　　　　　　　　　　　〕

🐾**Hints**
環境問題に対する考え方が変わったきっかけについて答えましょう。

😀 Production (Speaking)　自分の考えを話して伝えよう【思考力・判断力・表現力】　スピーキング・トレーナー

Answer the following question.　（9点）

What do you think we can do to protect the marine environment?　Refer to SDG Goal 14.

〔メ モ　　　　　　　　　　　　　　　　　　　　　　　　　　　　　　　〕

🐾**Hints**
SDGs の目標14「海の豊かさを守ろう」を参考に，海の環境を守るためにできることを考えましょう。

Bats and Gloves Instead of Bombs and Guns

In November 2006, / Mitsuru Okoso, / the leader of a Japanese NPO group, / received a letter / from his friend / Shoichi Ishida / in the U.S. // The letter said / a group of U.S. war **veterans** / wanted to play softball / against some Japanese veterans. // They had fought against Japan / in World War II. //

5　These veterans, / who were all 75 or older, / were members / of a world-**renowned** senior softball team / in Florida. // Ishida was a TV director / and had once made a documentary film / about the team. // One of the veterans told Ishida / about his wish / for the game, / and Ishida then asked Okoso / for his help. //

10　The man / who **originated** the idea / for the game / was Harvey Musser. // He had fought against Japan / on Leyte Island / during the war. // He got injured / in the left half of his body / and lost the sight / of his left eye / during the battle. // He said, / "We fought / in the war / but we do not hate the Japanese. // We want to fight with them again, / but this time, / through a softball game." //　　(174 words)

音読しよう 📖　　　　　　　　　　　　　　　　　　スピーキング・トレーナー

Practice 1 スラッシュ位置で文を区切って読んでみよう ☐
Practice 2 音声を聞きながら，音声のすぐ後を追って読んでみよう ☐
TRY! 1分30秒以内に本文全体を音読しよう ☐

📖 Reading 本文の内容を読んで理解しよう【知識・技能】【思考力・判断力・表現力】　　共通テスト GTEC®

Make the correct choice to complete each sentence or answer each question.　（各5点[(3)は完答]）

(1) What does "wish" mean in line 8? ☐
　① appetite　　　　② desire　　　　③ estimate　　　　④ wealth

(2) Members of the American softball team ☐.
　① had experienced the war
　② hoped to play softball with Japanese professional baseball players
　③ received a letter from Japanese veterans
　④ were born in Florida

(3) Put the following events (①～④) into the order in which they happened.
　☐ → ☐ → ☐ → ☐
　① Ishida asked Okoso for his help.
　② Ishida made a documentary film about the senior softball team in Florida.
　③ One of the U.S. veterans talked with Ishida about his wish.
　④ The U.S. veterans fought against Japan in World War II.

📝 Vocabulary & Grammar　重要表現や文法事項について理解しよう【知識】　　英検® GTEC®

Make the correct choice to complete each sentence.　（各3点）

(1) We must fight (　　　) any kind of discrimination.
　① above　　　　② against　　　　③ around　　　　④ at

(2) Some (　　　) commentators will be invited to the competition as judges.
　① renewed　　　② removed　　　③ renowned　　　④ restored

(3) The new technology (　　　) in Japan and quickly spread around the world.
　① origin　　　　② original　　　③ originality　　　④ originated

(4) He shares his experience with future generations as one of the World War II
　(　　　).
　① varieties　　　② veterans　　　③ vehicles　　　④ visions

(5) Sara (　　　) snow until she came to Japan.
　① doesn't see　　② hadn't been seen　③ hadn't seen　④ hasn't seen

🎧 Listening　英文を聞いて理解しよう【知識・技能】【思考力・判断力・表現力】　　共通テスト 🔵41

Listen to the English and make the best choice to match the content.　（4点）
　① Baseball is preferred to softball in Japan.
　② In the Taisho era, softball was introduced to Japan.
　③ The speaker likes playing softball with American veterans.

💬 Interaction　英文を聞いて会話を続けよう【知識・技能】【思考力・判断力・表現力】　　スピーキング・トレーナー

Listen to the English and respond to the remarks.　（7点）
　〔メ　モ　　　　　　　　　　　　　　　　　　　　　　　　　　　　　　　　　　〕

🔔 **Hints**
　家族や友人だけでなく，応援している有名人などについて答えても構いません。

😀💬 Production（Speaking）　自分の考えを話して伝えよう【思考力・判断力・表現力】　　スピーキング・トレーナー

Answer the following question.　（9点）

If you were over 75 years old, what sport would you like to do? Why?
　〔メ　モ　　　　　　　　　　　　　　　　　　　　　　　　　　　　　　　　　　〕

🔔 **Hints**
　自分が75歳以上だった場合，どんなスポーツがしたいか想像して話してみよう。

Okoso decided to help Ishida / and the veterans, / and started to look for Japanese senior players. // He needed at least 11 players, / but it was not an easy job / to find them. // He set up a website, / made a leaflet, / and asked newspaper companies / and TV stations / to report this news. // Soon / one

5 player after another / responded to Okoso's **plea**. //

One player had been a **suicide** attack **diver**. // He was about to die / at the end of the war. // Another had been a pilot / who had just barely escaped / from an attack / by American planes. // Still another had experienced an aerial bombing / by a B29 / and lost many friends. // All the players had gone through that

10 terrible war, / but now wanted to enjoy a softball game / with Americans. //

While gathering the members, / Okoso lost two of them / as they passed away / because of illness. // It was a sad experience / for him / and the other members. // However, / it **strengthened** his **determination** / to find a way / to successfully hold the game. // Finally, / he was able to find 19 players. //

(177 words)

))) 音読しよう

スピーキング・トレーナー

Practice 1 スラッシュ位置で文を区切って読んでみよう ☐

Practice 2 音声を聞きながら，音声のすぐ後を追って読んでみよう ☐

TRY! 1分35秒以内に本文全体を音読しよう ☐

📖 Reading 本文の内容を読んで理解しよう【知識・技能】【思考力・判断力・表現力】 共通テスト GTEC®

Make the correct choice to complete each sentence or answer each question. (各5点)

(1) What does "go through" mean in line 9? ☐

① accept ② compose ③ experience ④ protest

(2) All Japanese players ☐.

① had tragic experiences during the war, but now they were eager to play softball with Americans

② lost many friends because of aerial bombing during the war

③ wanted to play softball with Americans during the war

④ were pilots who had just barely escaped from an attack by American planes

(3) Finally, Okoso ☐.

① enjoyed playing softball with American veterans

② found more players than the required number of players

③ succeeded in defeating American players

④ watched Ishida's documentary film

Vocabulary & Grammar　重要表現や文法事項について理解しよう【知識】　英検® GTEC®

Make the correct choice to complete each sentence.　（各3点）

(1) In our customer service department, one of the rules is to (　　　) to customers' requests quickly.

① release　　　　② require　　　　③ respond　　　　④ restore

(2) When I arrived at the theater, the movie was (　　　) to start.

① about　　　　② above　　　　③ absent　　　　④ around

(3) Rick (　　　) his sense of responsibility because he became the leader of the group.

① strength　　② strengthened　　③ strong　　④ strongly

(4) The singer ignored the girl's (　　　) for his autograph.

① plea　　　　② pleasant　　　　③ please　　　　④ pleased

(5) Lucy has two sons. One lives in London and (　　　) lives in Paris.

① another　　② other　　③ the other　　④ the others

Listening　英文を聞いて理解しよう【知識・技能】【思考力・判断力・表現力】　共通テスト 🔘42

Listen to the English and make the best choice to match the content.　（4点）

① The leaders finished discussing the noise problem at military bases.

② The number of military bases in Okinawa is decreasing.

③ There seem to be some problems near military bases.

Interaction　英文を聞いて会話を続けよう【知識・技能】【思考力・判断力・表現力】　スピーキング・トレーナー

Listen to the English and respond to the remarks.　（7点）

〔メ モ　　　　　　　　　　　　　　　　　　　　　　　　　　　　　　　　　　　〕

🎧 **Hints**
自分の過去を振り返り，固い決意をした経験について話してみよう。

Production (Writing)　自分の考えを書いて伝えよう【思考力・判断力・表現力】

Write your answer to the following question.　（9点）

Write about your experience learning about wars.

🎧 **Hints**
平和学習や戦争について学んだ経験について書きましょう。

There were also other tasks / for Okoso / to do. // One was to find a stadium. // The location / of the game / was decided to be in Hawaii / as it is warm / and conveniently located / right between Japan and Florida. // Also, / it was the place / where the attack on **Pearl Harbor** occurred. // Okoso had difficulty

5　booking a stadium, / but finally found one. //

　　Another task was to decide the date. // November or December / was thought to be the best, / as the playing seasons / for both sides / **overlapped** / during that time. // Some U.S. veterans **suggested** / the game be on December 7, / when they had experienced the attack on Pearl Harbor / in the U.S. time. // However, / the

10　dates became December 18 and 19 / in 2007, / when the stadium was available. //

　　As the game was approaching, / Okoso found out / some of the U.S. members / had **canceled** their participation. // One said / he didn't feel like playing / with Japanese veterans / near Pearl Harbor. // Okoso realized / that there were still some people / in the U.S. / who saw the Japanese / as **villains**. //

(172 words)

音読しよう

Practice 1 スラッシュ位置で文を区切って読んでみよう ☐
Practice 2 音声を聞きながら，音声のすぐ後を追って読んでみよう ☐
TRY! 1分30秒以内に本文全体を音読しよう ☐

スピーキング・トレーナー

Reading　本文の内容を読んで理解しよう【知識・技能】【思考力・判断力・表現力】　　共通テスト

Make the correct choice to complete each sentence or answer each question. （各5点）

(1) Which of the following factors is **not** mentioned in deciding the stadium? ☐
　① climate　　② historical background　　③ location　　④ popularity

(2) Which of the following is true? ☐
　① November or December was thought to be the best because it was warm in both countries.
　② Okoso asked the U.S. members to have the game on the same day as the attack on Pearl Harbor.
　③ Some Japanese veterans suggested the game be on December 18 and 19.
　④ Some U.S. members hoped that the game would be held on December 7.

(3) Some of the U.S. veterans had canceled their participation because ☐ .
　① they found out that the Japanese team was so weak
　② they realized that there were still some people in Japan who saw the Americans as villains
　③ they still had a negative impression of Japanese people
　④ they were too nervous to play softball

意味の区切りを理解してスムーズに音読することができる。　試合開催までの苦労に関する英文を読んで概要や要点をとらえることができる。
文脈を理解して適切な語句を用いて英文を完成することができる。　平易な英語で話される短い英文を聞いて必要な情報を聞き取ることができる。
ドタキャンへの対応について簡単な語句を用いて情報や考えを伝えることができる。　戦争をテーマにした作品について簡単な語句を用いて考えを表現することができる。

Vocabulary & Grammar 重要表現や文法事項について理解しよう【知識】 英検® GTEC®

Make the correct choice to complete each sentence. （各3点）

(1) My room is on the second floor, so I always have (　　　) carrying my heavy luggage.

① ability 　　　② difficulty 　　　③ disability 　　　④ toughness

(2) Today's baseball game will be (　　　) because of the large typhoon.

① canceled 　　　② cleared 　　　③ compared 　　　④ completed

(3) At the meeting, our team leader asked us to (　　　) a new idea.

① suggest 　　　② supply 　　　③ suppose 　　　④ surround

(4) The woman wearing the (　　　) earrings over there is my sister.

① pearl 　　　② pile 　　　③ pinch 　　　④ prime

(5) Could you call us again at 11 a.m., (　　　) Lick will be back?

① that 　　　② what 　　　③ when 　　　④ which

Listening 英文を聞いて理解しよう【知識・技能】【思考力・判断力・表現力】 共通テスト　43

Listen to the English and make the best choice to match the content. （4点）

① The author of the story is a U.S. veteran.

② The speaker's parents owned a glass factory.

③ The story is based on the author's wartime experiences.

Interaction 英文を聞いて会話を続けよう【知識・技能】【思考力・判断力・表現力】 スピーキング・トレーナー

Listen to the English and respond to the last remark. （7点）

〔メモ 　　　　　　　　　　　　　　　　　　　　　　　　　　　　　　　　　　　〕

🎧 **Hints**
直前になって予定をキャンセルする人についてどう思うか，自分の意見を話してみよう。

Production (Writing) 自分の考えを書いて伝えよう【思考力・判断力・表現力】

Write your answer to the following question. （9点）

Write a brief summary or your opinion about a novel or movie that depicts war.

🎧 **Hints**
戦争を描いている小説や映画について，要約や感想を書きましょう。

Lesson 17

Bats and Gloves Instead of Bombs and Guns

Play for **Goodwill** / — American and Japanese veterans / make runs, / not war / in Waipahu. //

MORE THAN 60 years / after WWII, / veterans from the US and Japan / changed the **battlefield** / into the softball field. // Both teams / — 14 players / from Florida /
5 and 19 / from Japan / — **healed** old **wounds** / by playing softball together. //

The game was held / on December 19 / in Waipahu, / Hawaii. // It started / with 5 runs / by the US team / in the 1st **inning** / of the seven-inning game. // Though the Japanese fought back / in the 4th and 5th innings, / the US led the game / till the end. // The US won / with a final score of 14—2. //

10 After the game, / Mr. Yasukura, / an 84-year-old Japanese veteran, / laughed and said, / "We lost completely, / but I enjoyed the game. // I'm happy." // Mr. Devine, / an 82-year-old US veteran, / said, / "I couldn't think of a better way / for people / from two countries / to **patch** up old wounds / than to play softball together." // Players on both teams / used the game / to put the past behind /
15 and build an unforgettable friendship. //

(172 words)

音読しよう

スピーキング・トレーナー

Practice 1 スラッシュ位置で文を区切って読んでみよう ☐
Practice 2 音声を聞きながら，音声のすぐ後を追って読んでみよう ☐
TRY! 1分30秒以内に本文全体を音読しよう ☐

📖 Reading 本文の内容を読んで理解しよう【知識・技能】【思考力・判断力・表現力】

共通テスト GTEC®

Make the correct choice to complete each sentence or answer each question. (各5点)

(1) What does "heal" mean in line 5? ☐
　① cure　　　　② break　　　　③ leave　　　　④ kill

(2) Mr. Yasukura ☐ .
　① looked angry because the Japanese team had never led the game
　② looked happy because his team won the game
　③ said, "I couldn't think of a better way to patch up old wounds than to play softball together"
　④ seemed to be satisfied with the game although the Japanese team lost

(3) The softball game ☐ .
　① promoted friendship among the players from both teams
　② reminded the players of their sad memories from the war
　③ seemed to motivate some players to play the next game
　④ was the best way for all players to patch up their old wounds

Vocabulary & Grammar 重要表現や文法事項について理解しよう【知識】 (英検®) (GTEC®)

Make the correct choice to complete each sentence. （各3点）

(1) Mike had a big fight with Fred yesterday but they are trying to (　　) up their relationship now.

① clean   ② patch   ③ stand   ④ throw

(2) The government donated a large amount of money to the country as a gesture of (　　).

① good-looking   ② goodwill   ③ grave   ④ gravity

(3) My mother applied some cream to her hands to (　　) the damaged skin.

① harm   ② heal   ③ hesitate   ④ hospitalize

(4) It is said that the man died from (　　) he received in the battle.

① wallets   ② witnesses   ③ workforces   ④ wounds

(5) We seem to be surrounded by more enemies (　　) we realize.

① than   ② what   ③ where   ④ whose

Listening 英文を聞いて理解しよう【知識・技能】【思考力・判断力・表現力】 (共通テスト) 🔴44

Listen to the English and make the best choice to match the content. （4点）

① The listeners must use five colors to paint the picture.

② The players from five continents were united in the Olympic Games.

③ The speaker is delivering information related to the Olympics.

Interaction 英文を聞いて会話を続けよう【知識・技能】【思考力・判断力・表現力】 スピーキング・トレーナー

Listen to the English and respond to the last remark. （7点）

〔メ　モ 　　　　　　　　　　　　　　　　　　　　　　　　　　　　　　　　　　　　〕

🌡 **Hints**

嫌なことがあったときの対処法を話してみよう。

Production (Speaking) 自分の考えを話して伝えよう【思考力・判断力・表現力】 スピーキング・トレーナー

Answer the following question. （9点）

Who do you think promotes or promoted international goodwill?

〔メ　モ 　　　　　　　　　　　　　　　　　　　　　　　　　　　　　　　　　　　　〕

🌡 **Hints**

国際親善に努めている，もしくは努めたと思う人物について話しましょう。

Lesson 18 — "Brighten the World in Your Corner"

On December 4, / 2019, / the shocking news / of Dr. Tetsu Nakamura's death / traveled around the world. // Nakamura was shot dead / in a **gun** attack / while he was heading / for an **irrigation canal** project site. // Why was the **famed** Japanese doctor heading / for the irrigation canal site, / not a hospital? //

5 In 1984, / Nakamura was sent to Peshawar, / Pakistan as a physician. // Once Nakamura started / performing his medical treatment, / he realized / how limited medical resources were. // There were only 16 **sickbeds** / for 2,400 patients. // Essential medical instruments / like **stethoscopes** / were **totally lacking**. // He even carried his patients / on his back / because there were no **stretchers** / in 10 the hospital. //

By 1994, / Nakamura had established three clinics / in Afghanistan / to **expand** his treatment **capacity**. // In 2000, / a **catastrophic** drought struck Afghanistan, / leaving four million people / on the **verge** of starvation. // An increasing number of mothers / with dying children / visited Nakamura's clinics, / only to see 15 their children lose their lives / while waiting in line. // Nakamura cried out / to himself, / "If there were an adequate supply / of food and water, / these children could survive!" //

(178 words)

🔊 音読しよう 📖 ～～～～～～～～～～～～ スピーキング・トレーナー

Practice 1 スラッシュ位置で文を区切って読んでみよう ☐
Practice 2 音声を聞きながら，音声のすぐ後を追って読んでみよう ☐
TRY! 1分35秒以内に本文全体を音読しよう ☐

📖 Reading   本文の内容を読んで理解しよう【知識・技能】【思考力・判断力・表現力】   (共通テスト) (GTEC®)

Make the correct choice to answer each question.   (各5点[(3)は完答])

(1) What does "strike" mean in line 12? ☐
　① conflict　　　　② hit　　　　③ preserve　　　　④ terrify

(2) Which of the following is **not** true about the passage? ☐
　① In Peshawar, Pakistan, the medical resources available to Nakamura were very limited.
　② Nakamura had to carry his patients on his back due to the lack of stretchers.
　③ Nakamura was shot on his way to the irrigation canal project site.
　④ On December 4, 2019, Nakamura completed his journey around the world.

(3) Put the following events (①～④) into the order in which they happened.
　☐ → ☐ → ☐ → ☐
　① In Afghanistan, a severe drought occurred and many people suffered from starvation.
　② Nakamura started to work in Pakistan as a physician.
　③ Nakamura was killed on his way to the irrigation canal site.
　④ Three clinics were established by Nakamura in Afghanistan.

Vocabulary & Grammar　重要表現や文法事項について理解しよう【知識】　英検® GTEC®

Make the correct choice to complete each sentence.　（各3点）

(1)　Tim (　　　) for the kitchen to make breakfast after washing his face.
　　① faced　　　　② footed　　　　③ handed　　　　④ headed

(2)　It is reported that those butterflies are (　　　) of extinction.
　　① at the cost　　② in place　　　③ on the verge　　④ on top

(3)　The manufacturing facility will be (　　　) to increase production next year.
　　① erupted　　　② examined　　　③ expanded　　　④ exploded

(4)　Unfortunately, he (　　　) the confidence to speak to the girl he likes.
　　① lacks　　　　② links　　　　　③ locks　　　　　④ looks

(5)　If I (　　　) his phone number, I could call him right now.
　　① had known　　② have known　　③ knew　　　　④ known

Listening　英文を聞いて理解しよう【知識・技能】【思考力・判断力・表現力】　共通テスト　45

Listen to the English and make the best choice to match the content.　（4点）

　① All the terrorists involved in the September 11 terror attacks were arrested.
　② The leader of the September 11 terror attacks died during the attacks.
　③ The speaker is talking about the shocking terror attacks that occurred on September 11.

Interaction　英文を聞いて会話を続けよう【知識・技能】【思考力・判断力・表現力】　スピーキング・トレーナー

Listen to the English and respond to the last remark.　（7点）

〔メ モ　　　　　　　　　　　　　　　　　　　　　　　　　　　　　　　　　　　〕

🎧 Hints
なぜ干ばつが起こるのか説明してみよう。

Production (Writing)　自分の考えを書いて伝えよう【思考力・判断力・表現力】

Write your answer to the following question.　（9点）

Explain one thing you know about Pakistan or Afghanistan.

🎧 Hints
たとえば，アフガニスタンの首都はカブール(Kabul)，パキスタンの首都はイスラマバード(Islamabad)である。

Afghanistan was once a rich agricultural country. // However, / years of drought / as well as **continual** foreign invasion / changed everything. // Many villagers could no longer continue farming / and had to **abandon** their villages. // Nakamura believed / the country would never be **reconstructed** / without the
5 **revival** / of the abandoned farmland. //

Nakamura and his staff members / started to restore **dried**-up wells / and dig new wells. // It was **impossible** / to dig deeper into the wells / with human hands / because of a **layer** / of very large rocks. // **Therefore**, / they **scraped** out **explosive** materials / from unexploded bombs / and used them / to blow up the
10 rocks. // Thanks to their devoted work, / the total number of wells / had reached 1,600 / by 2006. //

Nakamura and his members / **launched** the "Green Ground Project." // The main part of the project / was the construction / of a 25-kilometer-long irrigation canal / named "Aab-e-Marwarid." //

15 Nakamura had to learn the basics / of canal construction. // He walked around / looking at irrigation facilities / not only in Afghanistan / but also in Japan. // After seven years of hardship, / the canal finally reached its **ultimate destination**, / the Gamberi **Desert**. //
(177 words)

🔊 **音読しよう** 📖 ～～～～～～ スピーキング・トレーナー

Practice 1 スラッシュ位置で文を区切って読んでみよう ☐
Practice 2 音声を聞きながら，音声のすぐ後を追って読んでみよう ☐
TRY! 1分35秒以内に本文全体を音読しよう ☐

📖 **Reading** 本文の内容を読んで理解しよう【知識・技能】【思考力・判断力・表現力】 （共通テスト）

Make the correct choice to complete each sentence or answer each question. （(1)は7点, (2)は8点）

(1) Which of the following is **not** true? ☐

① It took seven years to create some wells in the Gamberi Desert.

② Nakamura and his staff members used explosive materials when digging wells.

③ Nakamura visited some places to learn how to construct irrigation canals for the project.

④ One of the reasons villagers had to abandon their villages was continual foreign invasion.

(2) One **opinion** from the article is that ☐ .

① Afghanistan would not be reconstructed without the revival of the abandoned farmland

② Nakamura looked at irrigation facilities in both Afghanistan and Japan

③ the main part of the "Green Ground Project" was the construction of the "Aab-e-Marwarid"

④ the total number of wells had reached 1,600 by 2006

📝 Vocabulary & Grammar　重要表現や文法事項について理解しよう【知識】　英検® GTEC®

Make the correct choice to complete each sentence. （各3点）

(1) She (　　　) out the seeds of green peppers before frying them.

① figured　　　② ran　　　③ scraped　　　④ turned

(2) Although we got caught in a traffic jam, we were able to arrive at our (　　　) on schedule.

① departure　　　② destination　　　③ discovery　　　④ distance

(3) The (　　　) aim is not to achieve the goal, but to develop yourself by accomplishing it.

① affordable　　　② commercial　　　③ ultimate　　　④ unusual

(4) Finally, the bus service will be officially (　　　) next week at the request of the neighbors.

① caused　　　② competed　　　③ launched　　　④ suspected

(5) (　　　) him, we would not be able to solve this problem.

① Among　　　② Around　　　③ With　　　④ Without

🎧 Listening　英文を聞いて理解しよう【知識・技能】【思考力・判断力・表現力】　共通テスト　⭘46

Listen to the English and make the best choice to match the content. （4点）

① In the UAE, cucumbers are widely grown.

② It is mentioned that many farmers need salt in the UAE.

③ Japan is an agricultural country but there is a problem with farmers.

💬 Interaction　英文を聞いて会話を続けよう【知識・技能】【思考力・判断力・表現力】　スピーキング・トレーナー

Listen to the English and respond to the last remark. （7点）

〔メ モ 〕

🌡**Hints**
たとえば，スエズ運河(the Suez Canal)は紅海(the Red Sea)と地中海(the Mediterranean Sea)を結んでいる。

🗨 Production（Speaking）　自分の考えを話して伝えよう【思考力・判断力・表現力】　スピーキング・トレーナー

Answer the following question. （9点）

What abilities do you think leaders should have?

〔メ モ 〕

🌡**Hints**
ability (能力)，communication skill (コミュニケーション能力)，motivate (…をやる気にさせる)，strategy (戦略)

In 2003, / Nakamura received the Ramon Magsaysay Award, / which is **regarded** / as the Asian version / of the Nobel Prize. // In addition, / in 2019, / he was granted **honorary citizenship** / by the Afghan government / for his decades of **humanitarian** work / in the country. // In the same year, / however, / his **tragic**
5 **incident** happened. // Many people / in the world / **mourned** his sudden death. // Many Afghans / living in Japan / gathered / to show their deep **grief**. //

Peshawar-kai is an organization / which has supported Nakamura's work / physically and **spiritually**. // It was established / in 1983 / to back up his work / in Pakistan. // After Nakamura's death, / it declared / it would continue all the
10 work / he had **undertaken**. // The local staff regard themselves / as the students / of the Nakamura school / and share his **philosophy**, / "**Brighten** the world / in your corner." //

In the Gamberi Desert, / which was once feared / as the desert of death, / we can now see trees growing **thickly**. // We can also hear **songbirds chirping** /
15 and frogs **croaking**. // The Aab-e-Marwarid Canal / supports the **livelihoods** / of 600,000 farmers / in the area / along the canal / today. //

(175 words)

🔊)) 音読しよう 📖 ～～～～～～～～～～～～ スピーキング・トレーナー

Practice 1 スラッシュ位置で文を区切って読んでみよう ☐
Practice 2 音声を聞きながら，音声のすぐ後を追って読んでみよう ☐
TRY! 1分35秒以内に本文全体を音読しよう ☐

📖 **Reading** 本文の内容を読んで理解しよう【知識・技能】【思考力・判断力・表現力】 (共通テスト)

Make the correct choice to complete each sentence or answer each question. ((1)は完答8点, (2)は7点)

(1) Which of the following are true about the incidents in 2019? (Choose two options. The order does not matter.) ☐ · ☐

① Nakamura had the possibility of receiving the Nobel Prize.

② Nakamura passed away.

③ Nakamura received honorary citizenship from the Afghan government.

④ Nakamura received the Ramon Magsaysay Award.

⑤ Peshawar-kai was established to support Nakamura's work.

(2) Peshawar-kai ☐.

① announced that it would continue all of Nakamura's work

② has a lot of students who are studying Japanese to understand Nakamura's philosophy

③ is located in the Gamberi Desert

④ was an organization that supported Nakamura's work and ended its role with his death

Vocabulary & Grammar 重要表現や文法事項について理解しよう【知識】 (英検®) (GTEC®)

Make the correct choice to complete each sentence. （各3点）

(1) Katie (　　　　) Osaka as her home because she has lived there for 20 years.

　① appoints　　　② knows　　　③ regards　　　④ serves

(2) The (　　　) ending of this novel made me cry.

　① formal　　　② inaccurate　　　③ mutual　　　④ tragic

(3) Thank you so much!　Your message has (　　　) my spirits.

　① bright　　　② brightened　　　③ brightly　　　④ brought

(4) He lost his wife and was in (　　　).

　① cry　　　② grief　　　③ lonely　　　④ sad

(5) This new appliance will (　　　) you a lot of electricity.

　① save　　　② stock　　　③ suffer　　　④ suppose

Listening 英文を聞いて理解しよう【知識・技能】【思考力・判断力・表現力】 (共通テスト) 🔴47

Listen to the English and make the best choice to match the content. （4点）

　① Some researchers will be sent to Egypt to study dry weather.

　② The speaker is concerned about some animals in dry regions.

　③ Many parts of the world are turning into deserts.

Interaction 英文を聞いて会話を続けよう【知識・技能】【思考力・判断力・表現力】 (スピーキング・トレーナー)

Listen to the English and respond to the last remark. （7点）

〔メモ　　　　　　　　　　　　　　　　　　　　　　　　　　　　　　　　　　　　〕

🎧 **Hints**
inspect (…を点検する), repair (…を修理する), maintenance cost (維持費)

Production (Writing) 自分の考えを書いて伝えよう【思考力・判断力・表現力】

Write your answer to the following question. （9点）

Talk about one person who received the Nobel Prize and his or her achievement.

✏ **Hints**
ノーベル賞を受賞した人について書きましょう。

"Brighten the World in Your Corner"

Interviewer : Could you tell us / about your new song / "A **grain** of wheat — Moment—"? //

Sada : Yes. // I wrote this song / to **dedicate** to Tetsu Nakamura. // Many Afghans were suffering / from bitter **civil** wars / and devastating droughts. //

5　Nakamura worked there / as a physician / for over thirty years / and maintained / **merely** offering medical services / was insufficient. //

Interviewer : What do you mean / by "insufficient"? //

Sada : Well. // Nakamura believed / adequate food and water supplies / should come before medical care. // So, / he **constructed** an irrigation canal / under

10　the slogan, / "One canal / instead of 100 clinics." //

Interviewer : I see. // Have you met Dr. Nakamura before? //

Sada : Unfortunately, / no. // Since I knew some members of Peshawar-kai, / I had expected / I would see him someday. // So / I was really shocked / to hear / that a humanitarian like him / was shot dead / by an armed group. //

15　Though I couldn't have a chance / to talk with him **directly**, / I feel / as if he had helped me make this song. // I strongly believe / the seeds / he sowed / in Afghanistan / will continue to grow. // We will never forget his kind smile / and **noble soul.** //

(175 words)

🔊)) 音読しよう 📖 〜〜〜〜〜〜〜〜〜〜〜〜〜〜 スピーキング・トレーナー

Practice 1 スラッシュ位置で文を区切って読んでみよう ☐
Practice 2 音声を聞きながら，音声のすぐ後を追って読んでみよう ☐
TRY! 1分35秒以内に本文全体を音読しよう ☐

📖 **Reading** 本文の内容を読んで理解しよう【知識・技能】【思考力・判断力・表現力】 　共通テスト

Make the correct choice to complete each sentence. ((1)は7点，(2)は8点)

(1) The slogan "One canal instead of 100 clinics" means that ☐.

① in developed countries, at least 100 clinics are needed

② medical care is more insufficient than food and water

③ people need enough food and water in the first place

④ people should construct irrigation canals in all of the dry areas

(2) One **fact** from the interview is that ☐.

① in Afghanistan, merely providing medical services was not enough

② Sada knew some members of Peshawar-kai

③ the seeds Nakamura sowed in Afghanistan will continue to grow

④ we will never forget Nakamura's kind smile and noble soul

Vocabulary & Grammar 重要表現や文法事項について理解しよう【知識】 (英検®) (GTEC®)

Make the correct choice to complete each sentence. (各3点)

(1) My father often said to me, "Spending time with my family comes ( ) anything else."

① across ② after ③ before ④ to

(2) I wonder if a large bridge could be ( ) to connect the continents.

① commuted ② conflicted ③ constructed ④ contributed

(3) The government set a goal to double ( ) production after the war.

① gap ② grade ③ grain ④ grave

(4) This cheese was imported ( ) from Italy.

① almost ② directly ③ nearly ④ necessarily

(5) He screamed and ran away ( ) he had seen a ghost.

① as if ② even if ③ if ④ without

Listening 英文を聞いて理解しよう【知識・技能】【思考力・判断力・表現力】 (共通テスト) 💿48

Listen to the English and make the best choice to match the content. (4点)

① It is not easy to get tickets for Masashi Sada's concerts.

② Masashi Sada writes cheerful songs, but his personality is gloomy.

③ The speaker's grandmother knows Masashi Sada's songs and his character.

Interaction 英文を聞いて会話を続けよう【知識・技能】【思考力・判断力・表現力】 スピーキング・トレーナー

Listen to the English and respond to the remarks. (7点)

〔メ モ 〕

Hints
あなたの好きなミュージシャンについて話してみよう。

Production (Speaking) 自分の考えを話して伝えよう【思考力・判断力・表現力】 スピーキング・トレーナー

Answer the following question. (9点)

If you write a song, who will you dedicate it to?

〔メ モ 〕

Hints
自分が書いた曲を誰に捧げたいか考えてみよう。

Food is important / for our lives. // It provides us / with energy and **nutrition**. // However, / we have been facing many serious problems / related to food. //

For example, / the Food and Agriculture Organization (FAO) shows / that more than 820 million people, / one in every nine / on earth, / are suffering from
5 **hunger**. // On the other hand, / the world's annual food waste / amounts to 1.3 billion tons. // This is **roughly** a third of the total food production / in the world. // In addition, / many studies report / that climate change has had negative effects / on crop quality. // Moreover, / there is a growing need / to address the diversity / of **dietary** habits / such as **vegetarianism** and **veganism**. // Shortages
10 of human resources / in **primary** food-related industries / have also been a big challenge / for many years. //

"Food technology," / known as "FoodTech" / in Japan, / may be one of the promising solutions / to many of these problems. // It means applying science / to the production, / **distribution**, / **preparation** / and development / of food. // It
15 is expected / that the market size / of the FoodTech industry / will greatly increase / in the future. //

(175 words)

🔊)) 音読しよう   スピーキング・トレーナー

Practice 1 スラッシュ位置で文を区切って読んでみよう ☐
Practice 2 音声を聞きながら，音声のすぐ後を追って読んでみよう ☐
TRY! 1分35秒以内に本文全体を音読しよう ☐

📖 Reading 本文の内容を読んで理解しよう【知識・技能】【思考力・判断力・表現力】   共通テスト GTEC®

Make the correct choice to answer each question. （各5点）

(1) What does "promising" mean in line 13? ☐
  ① flexible   ② grateful   ③ hopeful   ④ impressive

(2) Which of the following is true? ☐
  ① A third of the world's population is suffering from hunger.
  ② Annual food waste in Japan amounts to 1.3 billion tons.
  ③ The number of people who are vegetarian and vegan is gradually decreasing.
  ④ There has been a labor shortage in primary food-related industries for many years.

(3) Which of the following is **not** true about "Food technology"? ☐
  ① It is expected to create effective solutions to food-related problems.
  ② It is known as "FoodTech" in Japan.
  ③ People believe that it will solve the problem of climate change.
  ④ The market size of the FoodTech industry will continue to grow.

Vocabulary & Grammar 重要表現や文法事項について理解しよう【知識】 (英検®) (GTEC®)

Make the correct choice to complete each sentence. （各3点）

(1) (　　　) children with an adequate education is one of our missions.
① Containing ② Donating ③ Gaining ④ Providing

(2) The research shows that global warming has had a devastating (　　　) on the environment in this area.
① account ② affect ③ effect ④ encounter

(3) It is said that poor (　　　) can cause dry skin.
① inspiration ② nutrition ③ observation ④ reproduction

(4) The new production (　　　) system will be established to ensure a better supply.
① disadvantage ② disappointing ③ distance ④ distribution

(5) How long have you (　　　) for a bus?
① been waited ② been waiting ③ wait ④ waiting

Listening 英文を聞いて理解しよう【知識・技能】【思考力・判断力・表現力】 (共通テスト) 49

Listen to the English and make the best choice to match the content. （4点）

① The speaker always enjoys having lunch with some friends.
② The speaker hates bamboo shoots because they taste bitter.
③ The speaker is talking about one of the pleasures of eating food.

Interaction 英文を聞いて会話を続けよう【知識・技能】【思考力・判断力・表現力】 スピーキング・トレーナー

Listen to the English and respond to the last remark. （7点）

〔メモ 　　　　　　　　　　　　　　　　　　　　　　　　　　　　　　　　 〕

Hints
stock (在庫), "best before" day (賞味期限), "consume by" date (消費期限)

Production (Writing) 自分の考えを書いて伝えよう【思考力・判断力・表現力】

Write your answer to the following question. （9点）

Why do you think the number of farmers has been decreasing in Japan?

_____

_____

Hints
aging problem (高齢化問題), agricultural equipment (農業機器), day off (休日), unstable (不安定な)

Lesson 19 Food Technology

Part 2
教科書 p.152-153   / 50

Food technology is **utilized** / in food production / in many ways. // First, / there is now a variety of agricultural **machinery**. // For example, / drones are used / to **spray** crops / with agricultural **chemicals**. // Remotely **operated** farm **tractors** / cultivate land. // Also, / some robots / with artificial intelligence /
5 harvest crops / by judging from their color or shape. // These kinds of technology / help solve the problem / of labor shortages / in food production industries. //

Second, / so-called "plant factories" / are now in operation / to grow food. // They do not need **vast** land or sunlight. // They are not influenced / by the
10 weather, / either. // LED light, / CO_2 **concentration** / and **temperature** / in plant factories / are **automatically** controlled / for **photosynthesis**. // Plant factories are an example / of ways / to deal with the problem / of climate change. //

Food technology is also used / in food distribution. // For instance, / restaurants can reduce food waste / by registering for services / on the Internet. //
15 One service helps restaurants / sell their surplus food / to general customers / at low prices. // Such services directly connect food / with consumers / on the Internet. // They are called "D2C" (direct-to-consumer) business models / and are only possible / through technology. //

(181 words)

音読しよう   スピーキング・トレーナー

Practice 1 スラッシュ位置で文を区切って読んでみよう ☐
Practice 2 音声を聞きながら，音声のすぐ後を追って読んでみよう ☐
TRY! 1分35秒以内に本文全体を音読しよう ☐

Reading 本文の内容を読んで理解しよう【知識・技能】【思考力・判断力・表現力】 (共通テスト)

Make the correct choice to answer each question. ((1)は7点, (2)は8点)

(1) Which of the following is **not** true? ☐
　① Drones are used to spray pesticides on crops.
　② LED light, CO_2 concentration and temperature in plant factories are controlled by engineers.
　③ Plant factories are not affected by weather conditions.
　④ Various types of machinery help to address labor shortages in food production industries.

(2) Which of the following is true about "D2C"? ☐
　① It is a service that directly connects food with consumers at shops.
　② It is one of the business models found in food distribution.
　③ It means that restaurants sell their surplus food to general customers at low prices.
　④ It refers to a service that restaurant sell their surplus food to other restaurants.

Vocabulary & Grammar 重要表現や文法事項について理解しよう【知識】　英検® GTEC®

Make the correct choice to complete each sentence. （各3点）

(1) Before entering the prize competition, you must (　　　　) for the application.

① recognize ② register ③ respond ④ revive

(2) This room is too small to put some furniture, so let's (　　　　) the dead space.

① underline ② unite ③ upload ④ utilize

(3) *A:* What's the suitable room (　　　) for dogs?

　B: It seems to be between 20 and 25 degrees.

① distance ② height ③ material ④ temperature

(4) This dashboard camera can start recording (　　　　) as soon as the engine is turned on.

① automatically ② extremely ③ finally ④ importantly

(5) The social events helped employees (　　　) to know each other better.

① get ② getting ③ got ④ have get

🎧 Listening 英文を聞いて理解しよう【知識・技能】【思考力・判断力・表現力】　共通テスト　💿50

Listen to the English and make the best choice to match the content. （4点）

① Growing apples is easier than growing peaches in Tohoku.

② Many farmers read the newspaper to check the weather.

③ Some farmers are changing the crops they grow because of global warming.

💬 Interaction 英文を聞いて会話を続けよう【知識・技能】【思考力・判断力・表現力】　スピーキング・トレーナー

Listen to the English and respond to the last remark. （7点）

〔メ モ　　　　　　　　　　　　　　　　　　　　　　　　　　　　　　　　　　　　　　〕

🔑 **Hints**
reduce working hours（作業時間を短縮する），safety（安全性），cost（費用），maintenance（メンテナンス）

💬 Production（Speaking） 自分の考えを話して伝えよう【思考力・判断力・表現力】　スピーキング・トレーナー

Answer the following question. （9点）

Give one example of FoodTech in food distribution.

〔メ モ　　　　　　　　　　　　　　　　　　　　　　　　　　　　　　　　　　　　　　〕

🔑 **Hints**
スマートフォンのアプリなどを活用したデリバリーサービスなども，食品流通におけるフードテックの一例である。

Lesson 19 Food Technology

Food technology also contributes / to food preparation. // Cooking methods / based on food technology / have been becoming popular recently. // For example, / you can **transform** cooking ingredients / into a **mousse**-formed **substance** / by adding CO₂. // This creates different **textures**. // You can also
5 **freeze** cooking ingredients **instantly** / with **liquid nitrogen** / to preserve their **flavor** and **freshness**. //

The "smart kitchen" still sounds **unfamiliar**, / but it may change the way / we cook / at home / in the near future. // This applies "IoT" (Internet of Things) / to cooking. // It connects recipes, / **grocery** shopping / and food preparation. //
10 First, / you select your favorite recipe / for your meal / on a special **app** / in your smartphone. // Next, / you order the ingredients / by tapping on them. // Then, / after the ingredients are delivered, / the smart kitchen will start / to help you cook / by controlling your kitchen appliances. // As a result, / the smart kitchen can gather various data / such as when and what you eat. // With such personal
15 data, / it will be able to help design an ideal **diet**. //

As **mentioned** above, / food technology is utilized / in food preparation / in many ways. // It will help people / enjoy making and eating their meals, / and become healthier. //

(190 words)

🔊)) **音読しよう** 📖 ～～～～～～～～～～～～～～～～ **スピーキング・トレーナー**

Practice 1 スラッシュ位置で文を区切って読んでみよう ☐
Practice 2 音声を聞きながら，音声のすぐ後を追って読んでみよう ☐
TRY! 1分40秒以内に本文全体を音読しよう ☐

📖 Reading 本文の内容を読んで理解しよう【知識・技能】【思考力・判断力・表現力】 （共通テスト）（GTEC®）

Make the correct choice to complete each sentence or answer each question. （各5点）

(1) What does "appliance" mean in line 13? ☐
　① application　　② device　　③ object　　④ option

(2) Which of the following is **not** true about a "smart kitchen"? ☐
　① It can collect personal information about what and when users eat.
　② It may change how to cook at restaurants in the near future.
　③ It applies "IoT" to cooking.
　④ Users can select a recipe on a special app.

(3) One **fact** from the article is that ☐ .
　① food technology is utilized in food preparation in many ways
　② food technology will help people become healthier
　③ food technology-based cooking methods have been gaining popularity
　④ the term "smart kitchen" still sounds unfamiliar

🏷 Vocabulary & Grammar   重要表現や文法事項について理解しよう【知識】   英検® GTEC®

Make the correct choice to complete each sentence.   (各3点)

(1) This is a new machine that can (   ) heat into electricity.
　　① transform　　　② translate　　　③ transport　　　④ trust

(2) He doesn't like sushi because of its (   ).
　　① technique　　　② texture　　　③ therapy　　　④ thumb

(3) (   ) hand soap is now more common than bar soap.
　　① Fluent　　　② Liquid　　　③ Solid　　　④ Tough

(4) Be more careful when driving on (   ) roads.
　　① unfamiliar　　　② unimportant　　　③ unnecessary　　　④ urgent

(5) Do you remember (   ) he said during the meeting?
　　① how　　　② what　　　③ which　　　④ who

🎧 Listening   英文を聞いて理解しよう【知識・技能】【思考力・判断力・表現力】   共通テスト 🔘 51

Listen to the English and make the best choice to match the content.   (4点)

① The speaker thinks "local production for local consumption" can be useful in many ways.

② The speaker took a class on how to grow vegetables.

③ Vegetable transportation costs are getting higher and higher.

💬 Interaction   英文を聞いて会話を続けよう【知識・技能】【思考力・判断力・表現力】   スピーキング・トレーナー

Listen to the English and respond to the last remark.   (7点)

〔メ モ　　　　　　　　　　　　　　　　　　　　　　　　　　　　　　　　　　　〕

🔑 **Hints**
スマートキッチンをみんなが使うべきかどうか考えてみよう。

✍ Production (Writing)   自分の考えを書いて伝えよう【思考力・判断力・表現力】

Write your answer to the following question.   (9点)

Give one example of FoodTech in food preparation.

🔑 **Hints**
食材や調味料を入れるだけで調理してくれる調理家電なども，食品の調理におけるフードテックの一例である。

Food Technology

A Imitation meat / and **cultured** meat //

Imitation meat is a meat-like product / produced from plants. // It is mainly made / from **soybeans**, / wheat, / **peas** / and so on. // It can address dietary diversity / such as vegetarianism and veganism. // Cultured meat is produced /
5 by culturing the cells / of animals / instead of killing them. // Both kinds of meat / taste just like real meat, / and they may be considered / better than **conventional** meat / in terms of ethical, / health, / environmental, / cultural / and economic aspects. //

B Insect food //

10 Some insects are **edible** / and high in **protein**. // Actually, / they have been **consumed** / as food / in some countries / for many years. // Popular species are grasshoppers, / **crickets**, / **beetles**, / bees, / and others. // Recently, / they are being processed / with technology / and made into various useful forms / such as powders, / **pastes**, / liquids / and oils. // Insect food can be mass-produced
15 sustainably / and is expected / to be a solution / to food **crises** and hunger. //

C Meal **replacement** //

Meal replacement refers to pre-**packaged** food meals. // It is full of **nutrients** / such as proteins, / fats, / fiber, / vitamins, / minerals / and **carbohydrates**. // It comes in various forms / such as powders, / bars, / drinks, / **etc.** // Meal
20 replacement products / are convenient **alternatives** / for healthy and low-calorie meals. //

(183 words)

 音読しよう

スピーキング・トレーナー

Practice 1 スラッシュ位置で文を区切って読んでみよう ☐
Practice 2 音声を聞きながら，音声のすぐ後を追って読んでみよう ☐
TRY! 1分35秒以内に本文全体を音読しよう ☐

📖 Reading　本文の内容を読んで理解しよう【知識・技能】【思考力・判断力・表現力】　共通テスト

Make the correct choice to complete each sentence or answer each question.　((1)は 7 点，(2)は 8 点)

(1) Which of the following is **not** true?　☐

① Both imitation meat and cultured meat are produced without killing animals.

② Grasshoppers are the most popular insects used for food.

③ Meal replacement is full of nutrients such as proteins, fats and so on.

④ Meal replacement is provided in various forms such as powders, bars, drinks, etc.

(2) One **fact** from the article is that　☐　.

① imitation meat is mainly made from soybeans, wheat, peas, and so on

② imitation meat and cultured meat taste just like real meat

③ insect food can be a solution to food crises and hunger

④ meal replacement products are convenient alternatives for healthy and low-calorie meals

Vocabulary & Grammar 重要表現や文法事項について理解しよう【知識】 (英検®) (GTEC®)

Make the correct choice to complete each sentence. （各3点）

(1) He always thinks about everything (   ) of money, so he is often avoided by others.

   ① a good deal   ② as a result   ③ in spite   ④ in terms

(2) Is this mushroom (   )? The color looks a little strange.

   ① edible   ② energetic   ③ enormous   ④ excused

(3) The country is facing an economic (   ).

   ① circle   ② clue   ③ crime   ④ crisis

(4) The (   ) to a traditional work style is remote or virtual work.

   ① alternative   ② argument   ③ atmosphere   ④ attempt

(5) Sorry! You can't use this restroom now. It is (   ).

   ① be cleaned   ② being cleaned   ③ being cleaning   ④ cleaning

🎧 Listening 英文を聞いて理解しよう【知識・技能】【思考力・判断力・表現力】 (共通テスト) ◎52

Listen to the English and make the best choice to match the content. （4点）

   ① For people in Nagano, eating insects is one way to get protein.

   ② People in Nagano think insect food is healthier than seafood.

   ③ There are some dangerous insects in the forest in Nagano.

💬 Interaction 英文を聞いて会話を続けよう【知識・技能】【思考力・判断力・表現力】 (スピーキング・トレーナー)

Listen to the English and respond to the remarks. （7点）

〔メモ   〕

🔑 Hints
培養肉の利点を話しましょう。

🗨 Production (Speaking) 自分の考えを話して伝えよう【思考力・判断力・表現力】 (スピーキング・トレーナー)

Answer the following question. （9点）

Point out one problem related to imitation meat, cultured meat, insect food, or meal replacements.

〔メモ   〕

🔑 Hints
代替食品や昆虫食の問題点を指摘してみよう。

Now, / let me give you three examples / of global issues / facing the world today. // First, / we often hear news / like "We had the most devastating flood / in a century." // In fact, / climate change has become so serious / that it can be referred to / as the "climate crisis." // Second, / unfortunately, / hunger and

5 **poverty** / in developing countries / still remain as huge barriers / to sustainable development. // According to the United Nations, / every year / about six million children / die from hunger and poor nutrition. // The third example is the issue of education. // We have to face the fact / that hundreds of millions of children / around the world / are unable to attend school. //

10 As you know, / there is no time / to lose / in tackling these global issues. // That's why the UN has adopted the 17 Sustainable Development Goals / — the SDGs. // They are a **blueprint** / for peace and **prosperity** / for people and the planet, / now and into the future. // They are an urgent call / to action / by all countries / in a global **partnership**. //

15 Now is the time / to consider what we can do / as individuals. // It is not enough / for us / to understand what the issues are. // We must transform the world / through our daily actions. //

(200 words)

🔊 **音読しよう** 📖 〜〜〜〜〜〜〜〜〜〜〜〜〜〜 スピーキング・トレーナー

Practice 1 スラッシュ位置で文を区切って読んでみよう ☐
Practice 2 音声を聞きながら，音声のすぐ後を追って読んでみよう ☐
TRY! 1分45秒以内に本文全体を音読しよう ☐

📖 **Reading** 本文の内容を読んで理解しよう【知識・技能】【思考力・判断力・表現力】 (共通テスト)

Make the correct choice to complete each sentence or answer each question. （(1)は7点, (2)は8点）

(1) Which of the following is **not** true? ☐
① David spoke about global issues such as climate change, hunger, and education.
② In developing countries, devastating floods are huge barriers to sustainable development.
③ The SDGs are a plan for peace and prosperity for the Earth, both now and in the future.
④ There are hundreds of millions of children who cannot attend school.

(2) One **fact** from the article is that ☐ .
① about six million children die from hunger and poor nutrition every year
② it is not enough for us to understand what the global issues facing the world today are
③ there is no time to set up rules for global issues
④ we have to consider the fact that many children around the world cannot attend school

Vocabulary & Grammar 重要表現や文法事項について理解しよう【知識】 英検® GTEC®

Make the correct choice to complete each sentence. （各 3 点）

(1) It was officially announced that a patient died (　　　) the side effects of the medicine.

　① down 　　　　② from 　　　　③ in 　　　　④ out

(2) Thanks to sustainable development, the country's (　　　) rate is decreasing.

　① bravery 　　　② gender 　　　③ machinery 　　　④ poverty

(3) He created a (　　　) for his future when he was a junior high school student.

　① blueprint 　　② border 　　　③ branch 　　　④ building

(4) The experts advised that more (　　　) between the two regions should be established.

　① airships 　　　② memberships 　　③ partnerships 　　④ scholarships

(5) I heard the news (　　　) there was a forest fire near the railway track.

　① that 　　　　② what 　　　　③ which 　　　　④ whose

Listening 英文を聞いて理解しよう【知識・技能】【思考力・判断力・表現力】 共通テスト 🔘 53

Listen to the English and make the best choice to match the content. （4 点）

　① Norway has several kinds of renewable energy power sources.

　② The speaker believes that nuclear power is necessary in the world.

　③ The speaker is concerned about the safety of the power plants.

Interaction 英文を聞いて会話を続けよう【知識・技能】【思考力・判断力・表現力】 スピーキング・トレーナー

Listen to the English and respond to the last remark. （7 点）

〔メモ 　　　　　　　　　　　　　　　　　　　　　　　　　　　　　　　　　　　〕

🎧 **Hints**
他人に行動を促す方法を話してみよう。

Production (Writing) 自分の考えを書いて伝えよう【思考力・判断力・表現力】

Write your answer to the following question. （9 点）

What do you think the world will be like after achieving the goals of the SDGs?

🎧 **Hints**
SDGs の目標が達成できたら，どのような世界が待っているのかを想像して書いてみよう。

I'd like to talk about SDG Goal 4, / "Quality Education." // I think / education is the most important thing / to improve our society. // This SDG's goal is / to make sure / that everyone can equally get a good education. // Education enables us / to live on our own / and escape poverty. // I have learned / that a

5 large number of children / around the world / cannot attend school. // I'm very shocked / to know this reality. // I'm wondering what we can do / as individuals. //

I want to introduce the "World TERAKOYA Movement (WTM)." // In 1989, / a Japanese NGO started it / as an international cooperation program / for education. // The main **objective** / of the WTM / is to provide **illiterate** adults and out-of-school

10 children / with opportunities / to receive an education. // I am impressed / by the goal / of the WTM: / to end the **cycle** / of poverty and **illiteracy**. //

On its website, / I heard a TERAKOYA student say, / "I'm very happy / that I was able to write my name / for the first time / in my life." // My future dream is / to be a teacher. // I hope to teach children / living in **harsh** conditions / like

15 him / someday. // (185 words)

🔊)) 音読しよう 📖 ～～～～～～～～～～ スピーキング・トレーナー

Practice 1 スラッシュ位置で文を区切って読んでみよう ☐
Practice 2 音声を聞きながら，音声のすぐ後を追って読んでみよう ☐
TRY! 1分40秒以内に本文全体を音読しよう ☐

📖 **Reading** 本文の内容を読んで理解しよう【知識・技能】【思考力・判断力・表現力】 共通テスト GTEC®

Make the correct choice to complete each sentence or answer each question. （各5点）

(1) What does "objective" mean in line 9? ☐
　① alternative　　② collection　　③ requirement　　④ target

(2) Manabu thinks that ☐.
　① all children should learn about SDG Goal 4
　② education is a key to escape poverty
　③ education is the second most important thing to improve society
　④ people in developed countries should get a good education equally

(3) Which of the following is true about "World TERAKOYA Movement (WTM)"? ☐
　① A Japanese NGO began it as an international cooperation program for poverty issues.
　② It aims to stop the cycle of poverty and illiteracy.
　③ It was started by a Japanese educational company.
　④ Its main objective is to provide educational opportunities for Japanese children.

📇 Vocabulary & Grammar　重要表現や文法事項について理解しよう【知識】　英検® GTEC®

Make the correct choice to complete each sentence.　（各3点）

(1) Please make (　　　　) that all the windows and doors are closed before leaving.

　① brief　　　　　② note　　　　　③ secure　　　　　④ sure

(2) The main (　　　　) is not to pass the test, but to improve study skills.

　① attractive　　　② competitive　　　③ objective　　　④ preventive

(3) (　　　　) prevents people from obtaining information.

　① Illiteracy　　　② Illustration　　　③ Influence　　　④ Innovation

(4) Domestic violence tends to follow a specific pattern known as the "(　　　　)" of violence."

　① cycle　　　　　② line　　　　　　③ square　　　　　④ triangle

(5) The development of technology (　　　　) people to live long and comfortable lives.

　① enables　　　　② keeps　　　　　③ makes　　　　　④ succeeds

🎧 Listening　英文を聞いて理解しよう【知識・技能】【思考力・判断力・表現力】　共通テスト 🔘54

Listen to the English and make the best choice to match the content.　（4点）

　① Literacy rates are gradually increasing each year.

　② There are still a lot of illiterate people in the world.

　③ There aren't any elementary schools in sub-Saharan countries.

💬 Interaction　英文を聞いて会話を続けよう【知識・技能】【思考力・判断力・表現力】　スピーキング・トレーナー

Listen to the English and respond to the last remark.　（7点）

　〔メモ　　　　　　　　　　　　　　　　　　　　　　　　　　　　　　　〕

🎙️ **Hints**

　寺子屋について話してみよう。

🗣️ Production (Speaking)　自分の考えを話して伝えよう【思考力・判断力・表現力】　スピーキング・トレーナー

Answer the following question.　（9点）

What do you think is needed to achieve SDG Goal 4?

　〔メモ　　　　　　　　　　　　　　　　　　　　　　　　　　　　　　　〕

🎙️ **Hints**

　SDGs の目標4「質の高い教育をみんなに」を達成するために必要だと思うものを話しましょう。

What I am most interested in / is SDG Goal 7. // Its purpose is to provide people / with affordable, **reliable**, sustainable and clean energy. // For many years, / **fossil fuels** have been the major energy resource. // But / burning fossil fuels / has been producing large amounts of **greenhouse** gases. // They have
5 caused climate change / and have had harmful impacts / on the environment. //

Let me tell you about Norway. // Surprisingly, / in Norway, / almost 100% of all electricity production / comes from **renewables**, / for the most part **hydropower**. // Norway's energy policy may be a special case, / but it's a good model / for our country. // As you know, / Japan is trying to increase the use of
10 renewables, / but their percentage will only increase / from 18% / to over 30% / by 2030. //

Don't you think / it is time / to take urgent action / to **shift** from fossil fuels / to renewables? // However, / the world, / especially many developing countries, / will need more and more energy / to develop their economies. // It is a great
15 challenge / to meet all the potential energy needs / only by using clean energy **sources**. // No matter how difficult it is, / we must do it / to preserve the earth / for future generations. //

(192 words)

🔊)) **音読しよう** 📖   スピーキング・トレーナー

Practice 1 スラッシュ位置で文を区切って読んでみよう ☐
Practice 2 音声を聞きながら，音声のすぐ後を追って読んでみよう ☐
TRY! 1分40秒以内に本文全体を音読しよう ☐

📖 **Reading** 本文の内容を読んで理解しよう【知識・技能】【思考力・判断力・表現力】   共通テスト

Make the correct choice to complete each sentence or answer each question. ((1)は完答8点, (2)は7点)

(1) Which of the following are true? (Choose two options. The order does not matter.)
☐ · ☐

① Fossil fuels are no longer used by any countries because they are harmful to the environment.
② In Norway, hydropower energy has been mainly used.
③ In Norway, nearly 100% of all electricity production comes from burning fossil fuels.
④ Japanese energy policy was the same as Norway's one before.
⑤ One of the purposes of SDG Goal 7 is to provide people with eco-friendly energy.

(2) One **fact** from the article is that ☐ .

① burning fossil fuels has been producing large amounts of greenhouse gases
② many developing countries will need more energy for economic growth
③ Norway's energy policy may be a special case
④ we must use clean energy to preserve the earth for future generations

Vocabulary & Grammar 重要表現や文法事項について理解しよう【知識】 (英検®) (GTEC®)

Make the correct choice to complete each sentence. （各3点）

(1) No matter (　　　　) long it takes, Mark will not give up.

① how ② what ③ when ④ who

(2) Do you think the information in this letter is (　　　　)?

① rather ② registered ③ reliable ④ relying

(3) The two countries agreed to reduce the use of (　　　　) fuels to address global warming.

① fire ② flood ③ fossil ④ storm

(4) The large corporations have been asked to reduce (　　　　) gas emissions from their factories.

① evil ② greenhouse ③ harm ④ negative

(5) My grandparents (　　　　) in this house for more than 50 years.

① have been lived ② have been living ③ lives ④ living

Listening 英文を聞いて理解しよう【知識・技能】【思考力・判断力・表現力】 (共通テスト) 💿 55

Listen to the English and make the best choice to match the content. （4点）

① Both Denmark and Norway are among the world's leading renewable energy producers.

② Norway produces more electricity from renewable energy sources than Denmark.

③ The speaker believes that hydropower is better than wind power.

Interaction 英文を聞いて会話を続けよう【知識・技能】【思考力・判断力・表現力】 スピーキング・トレーナー

Listen to the English and respond to the last remark. （7点）

〔メ　モ 　　　　　　　　　　　　　　　　　　　　　　　　　　　　　　　　　　　　　〕

Hints
日本で再生可能エネルギーへの転換が遅れている理由を話してみよう。

Production（Writing） 自分の考えを書いて伝えよう【思考力・判断力・表現力】

Write your answer to the following question. （9点）

What do you think we can do to achieve SDG Goal 7?

Hints
SDGsの目標7「エネルギーをみんなに そしてクリーンに」を達成するためにできることを考えましょう。

Lesson 20 Transforming Our World

I'd like to take up SDG Goal 1 / and SDG Goal 3. // SDG Goal 1, / "No Poverty," / is to end poverty / in all its forms / everywhere / by 2030. // SDG Goal 3, / "Good Health and Well-being," / aims to **ensure** healthy lives / and promote well-being / for all people / of all ages. //

5 SDG Goals 1 and 3 / are strongly **interconnected**. // In other words, / "No Poverty" is closely linked / to good health. // In fact, / people living in **extreme** poverty / cannot **fulfill** their most basic needs / like good health. // Have you ever heard / of "Doctors Without **Borders**"? // It is an international medical humanitarian organization / founded / in 1971 / in Paris. // It provides basic

10 medical care / for people / affected by war, / **epidemics** / or disasters. // I am impressed / that it is trying to realize SDG Goals 1 and 3. //

My future dream, / if possible, / is to work / as a volunteer / for "Doctors Without Borders." // The organization is made up of people / with diverse backgrounds / from all over the world. // The experience / of working with such

15 people / would **definitely** be a precious opportunity / for me, / and I would be happy / to contribute to the achievement / of the goals / of the SDGs. // (193 words)

🔊)) 音読しよう 📖 ⌇ スピーキング・トレーナー

Practice 1 スラッシュ位置で文を区切って読んでみよう ☐
Practice 2 音声を聞きながら，音声のすぐ後を追って読んでみよう ☐
TRY! 1分45秒以内に本文全体を音読しよう ☐

📖 **Reading** 本文の内容を読んで理解しよう【知識・技能】【思考力・判断力・表現力】 共通テスト GTEC®

Make the correct choice to complete each sentence or answer each question. （各5点）

(1) What does "diverse" mean in line 13? ☐
　① challenging　　② domestic　　③ international　　④ various

(2) Which of the following is **not** true about "Doctors Without Borders"? ☐
　① It is an international organization established in 1971.
　② It is attempting to achieve both SDG Goals 1 and 3.
　③ It provides high-quality operations for people injured during war.
　④ The organization has people with diverse backgrounds from around the world.

(3) One **fact** from the article is that ☐ .
　① contributing to the achievement of the goals of the SDGs would bring happiness
　② SDG Goal 3 aims to ensure that all people of all ages live healthy lives
　③ the work of "Doctors Without Borders" is impressive
　④ working with people from diverse backgrounds would be a valuable opportunity

Vocabulary & Grammar　重要表現や文法事項について理解しよう【知識】　英検® GTEC®

Make the correct choice to complete each sentence. （各3点）

(1) Our leader took (　　　) Ted's suggestion at the end of the meeting.
　　① in　　　　　　② off　　　　　　③ on　　　　　　④ up

(2) This committee is made up (　　　) eight experts.
　　① away　　　　　② for　　　　　　③ of　　　　　　④ on

(3) The local government has decided to provide free (　　　) for children as part of social welfare.
　　① hardship　　　② healthcare　　　③ honor　　　　④ hospitality

(4) The airline company must (　　　) the personal safety of its passengers.
　　① allow　　　　　② donate　　　　　③ ensure　　　　④ suppose

(5) (　　　) it be possible to take pictures here?
　　① If　　　　　　② May　　　　　　③ Whether　　　④ Would

🎧 Listening　英文を聞いて理解しよう【知識・技能】【思考力・判断力・表現力】　共通テスト　💿56

Listen to the English and make the best choice to match the content. （4点）

① The speaker is calling for donations to "Doctors Without Borders."

② The speaker is talking about basic information of the medical organization.

③ The speaker received the Nobel Peace Prize in 1999.

💬 Interaction　英文を聞いて会話を続けよう【知識・技能】【思考力・判断力・表現力】　スピーキング・トレーナー

Listen to the English and respond to the last remark. （7点）

〔メモ　　　　　　　　　　　　　　　　　　　　　　　　　　　　　　　　　　　　　　　〕

👆**Hints**
赤十字は，世界191か国に拠点を持つ国際組織で，被災地での医療や看護の支援などをおこなっています。

🗨️ Production (Speaking)　自分の考えを話して伝えよう【思考力・判断力・表現力】　スピーキング・トレーナー

Answer the following question. （9点）

What are you working on or planning to do to achieve SDG Goals 1 or 3?

〔メモ　　　　　　　　　　　　　　　　　　　　　　　　　　　　　　　　　　　　　　　〕

👆**Hints**
SDGsの目標1「貧困をなくそう」や目標3「すべての人に健康と福祉を」を達成するためにできることを考えましょう。

WPM・得点一覧表

●スピーキング・トレーナーを使って，各レッスンの本文を流暢に音読できるようにしましょう。
下の計算式を使って，1分あたりに音読できた語数 (words per minute) を算出してみましょう。

【本文語数】÷【音読にかかった時間 (秒)】×60＝□wpm

Unit 1

Lesson		WPM	得点
1	Get Ready	/ wpm	/ 50
	Practice	/ wpm	/ 50
	流暢さの目安	80wpm	/ 100
2	Get Ready	/ wpm	/ 50
	Practice	/ wpm	/ 50
	流暢さの目安	80wpm	/ 100
3	Get Ready	/ wpm	/ 50
	Practice	/ wpm	/ 50
	流暢さの目安	80wpm	/ 100
4	Get Ready	/ wpm	/ 50
	Practice	/ wpm	/ 50
	流暢さの目安	80wpm	/ 100
5	Get Ready	/ wpm	/ 50
	Practice	/ wpm	/ 50
	流暢さの目安	80wpm	/ 100
6	Get Ready	/ wpm	/ 50
	Practice	/ wpm	/ 50
	流暢さの目安	90wpm	/ 100
7	Get Ready	/ wpm	/ 50
	Practice	/ wpm	/ 50
	流暢さの目安	90wpm	/ 100
8	Get Ready	/ wpm	/ 50
	Practice	/ wpm	/ 50
	流暢さの目安	90wpm	/ 100

Lesson		WPM	得点
9	Get Ready	/ wpm	/ 50
	Practice	/ wpm	/ 50
	流暢さの目安	90wpm	/ 100
10	Get Ready	/ wpm	/ 50
	Practice	/ wpm	/ 50
	流暢さの目安	90wpm	/ 100

Unit 2

Lesson		WPM	得点
11	Part 1	/ wpm	/ 50
	Part 2	/ wpm	/ 50
	Part 3	/ wpm	/ 50
	流暢さの目安	100wpm	/ 150
12	Part 1	/ wpm	/ 50
	Part 2	/ wpm	/ 50
	Part 3	/ wpm	/ 50
	流暢さの目安	100wpm	/ 150
13	Part 1	/ wpm	/ 50
	Part 2	/ wpm	/ 50
	Part 3	/ wpm	/ 50
	流暢さの目安	100wpm	/ 150
14	Part 1	/ wpm	/ 50
	Part 2	/ wpm	/ 50
	Part 3	/ wpm	/ 50
	流暢さの目安	100wpm	/ 150
15	Part 1	/ wpm	/ 50
	Part 2	/ wpm	/ 50
	Part 3	/ wpm	/ 50
	流暢さの目安	100wpm	/ 150

Unit 3		
Lesson	**WPM**	**得点**
Part 1	/ wpm	/ 50
Part 2	/ wpm	/ 50
Part 3	/ wpm	/ 50
Part 4	/ wpm	/ 50
流暢さの目安	110wpm	/ 200
Lesson	**WPM**	**得点**
Part 1	/ wpm	/ 50
Part 2	/ wpm	/ 50
Part 3	/ wpm	/ 50
Part 4	/ wpm	/ 50
流暢さの目安	110wpm	/ 200
Lesson	**WPM**	**得点**
Part 1	/ wpm	/ 50
Part 2	/ wpm	/ 50
Part 3	/ wpm	/ 50
Part 4	/ wpm	/ 50
流暢さの目安	110wpm	/ 200
Lesson	**WPM**	**得点**
Part 1	/ wpm	/ 50
Part 2	/ wpm	/ 50
Part 3	/ wpm	/ 50
Part 4	/ wpm	/ 50
流暢さの目安	110wpm	/ 200
Lesson	**WPM**	**得点**
Part 1	/ wpm	/ 50
Part 2	/ wpm	/ 50
Part 3	/ wpm	/ 50
Part 4	/ wpm	/ 50
流暢さの目安	110wpm	/ 200

16
17
18
19
20